YORK
Through the Lens of
The Press

PAUL CHRYSTAL

December 1999: veteran news vendor Les Richardson with the final *Evening Press* before the year 2000

First Edition 2022

ISBN 978 1 7398194 1 5

Text 2022 © Paul Chrystal
Images © The Press unless stated otherwise

British Library Cataloguing-in-Publication Data
A catalogue record for this book is available from the British Library.

Published by Destinworld Publishing Ltd.
www.destinworld.com

Cover design by Ken Leeder showing Bowes Morrell House, 111 Walmgate Along with William Etty and WA Evelyn we have much to thank JB Morrell (1873-1963) for when it comes to saving York and its buildings from mindless destruction. Invaluable work for York Conservation Trust (which he co-founded) apart, Morrell was a director at Rowntree's from age twenty-five, Lord Mayor twice (in 1914 and 1950) and a powerful voice in the establishment of the University of York. The library there is named after him.

Printed and bound in the United Kingdom by Short Run Press

PREFACE

It is 810 years since King John granted a Royal Charter in 1212 allowing York political self-determination and trading practices controlled by the guilds. How the citizens of York deployed these rights has shaped and influenced York's history and heritage to this day. Richard II (1367 – 1400) came to York many times and granted the city greater freedoms and privileges. Most importantly, in 1396 he gave the city its most significant royal charter, which promoted it to the status of a county in its own right: 'the county of the city of York'. It starts:

Richard, by the grace of God King of England and France and Lord of Ireland, to his archbishops, bishops, abbots, priors, dukes, earls, barons, justices, sheriffs, reeves, officers, and all his bailiffs and loyal subjects, greetings. Know that by our special grace and at the petition of our well-loved subjects, the mayor and citizens of our city of York, we have granted and given licence, on behalf of ourself and our heirs (insofar as we may), to the mayor and citizens that they, their heirs and successors may acquire and hold in their name lands, tenements and rents with appurtenances up to the value of £100 annually, to be held of us in burgage within our city and its suburbs.

In 1920 George VI, then Duke of York, received the freedom of the city and declared that the *history of York is the history of England*'. Even allowing for regal hyperbole his observation confirms just how rich, deep and extensive the history of York is. If it does not match precisely the history of our nation then York's history and heritage certainly reflects and informs it in many different ways. This book will help to show how it does that, informing and entertaining visitor and resident alike.

This book is a unique compilation of around 275 photographs complete with captions which have been published in *The Press* (and before that *The Yorkshire Evening Press*) over the last 80 or so years. It is unique because this is the first time *The Press* has published a compilation of its finest pictures and because the book provides a fascinating pictorial history of York with images unobtainable from any other source. Captions accompany each of the photographs telling the story behind the picture, and placing it in historical context.

Many of the images have not been seen since they were first published in the *Press*, and for that reason they provide the reader an opportunity to indulge in some unashamed and untrammelled nostalgia, whatever their age. *York: Through the Lens…* will be sought after by York residents past and present, visitors, local historians and anyone interested in the history of the city and, indeed, of England.

Paul Chrystal, York, August 2022

Richard II's charter being shown in 1971 in York City Archive.

CONTENTS

ABOUT THE AUTHOR

Paul Chrystal has classics degrees from the universities of Hull and Southampton; he is the author of 120 or so published books, many of which are on York and Yorkshire. He has written features on aspects of the history of food and drink for the *Daily Express;* his *A History of Sweets* was serialised in the *Daily Mail* in June 2021. Paul has appeared on the BBC World Service, Radio 4's PM programme, talkRADIO and various BBC local radio stations speaking on a wide range of subjects. Paul has also contributed to a six-part series for BBC2 'celebrating the history of some of Britain's most iconic craft industries' – in this case chocolate in York, which aired in 2019 and was part of the research team for a 2022 episode of *Who Do You Think You Are?* He has been history advisor for a number of York tourist attractions. He is past editor of *York Historian* and past history editor of the *Yorkshire Archaeological Journal.* In 2019 he was guest speaker for the Vassar College (New York) London Programme with Goldsmith University. He was commissioned in 2022 to write a piece for Mars Confectionery UK celebrating their 90 years in the UK, he gives talks in schools; his books have been translated into Chinese and Japanese.

For a full list of his publications search www.paulchrystal.com

Banner in Station Road, 1988. Sign of the times

ACKNOWLEDGEMENTS

Thanks to Steve Lewis at *The Press* for making this happen, and to Odele Ayres, Nostalgia Writer & Researcher who painstakingly scanned all of the photographs.

This is how Daniel Defoe generously described York in his '*A Tour Thro' The Whole Island Of Great Britain*', 1724. No southern bias there.

> '*There is abundance of good company here, and abundance of good families live here, for the sake of the good company and cheap living; a man converses here with all the world as effectually as at London.*'

York's beautiful walls.

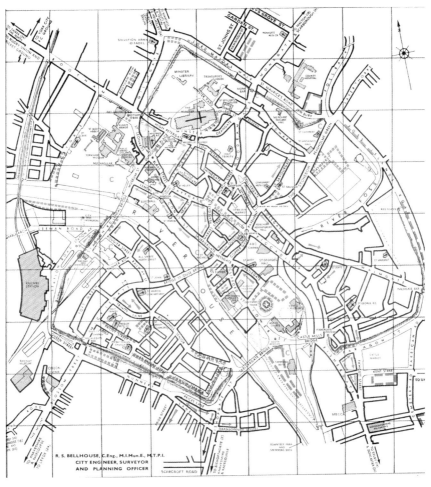

York in 1923. John Bartholomew & Co Edinburgh

INTRODUCTION

So, what sort of place was York, from the 17th century onwards? Industry, business and the people engaged therein define and shape a town or city and imbue it with much of its character. York is no exception, although its ecclesiastical heritage and high status in the Anglican church, its sheer historicity and its splendour and beauty also contribute to its reputation as one of the finest, most historical cities in Europe.

In the second half of the fourteenth century York, on account of its cloth trade and the ancillary industries associated with it, had been described as 'the foremost industrial town in the North of England.' This did not last, and the trade in cloth declined to such a degree that a visitor to the city in the seventeenth century, Thomas Fuller, harshly remarked: 'the foreign trade is like their river...low and flat.'

According to Francis Drake, in his *Eboracum: or the History and Antiquities of the City of York,* York in the eighteenth century had precious little industry and the only real commercial activity was butter exports, corn and wine trading. Defoe, in *A Tour Through the Whole Island of Great Britain* agrees: 'here is no trade...except such as depends upon the confluence of the gentry.' This was due in some extent both to the high price of coal in York which had to be shipped from the coalfields of the West Riding, and to the restrictive, exclusive attitude of the local guilds, particularly the Merchant Adventurers and their insistence that the freedom regulations, whereby all traders had to be freemen of the City, be rigorously observed. Moreover, up until 1827 when a judgement went against them, it seems that only members of the Merchant Adventurers' Company could carry out trade in imported goods. But the high price of coal would only really affect any heavy industry and the strictures of the Merchant Adventurers would not have impeded development and progress amongst

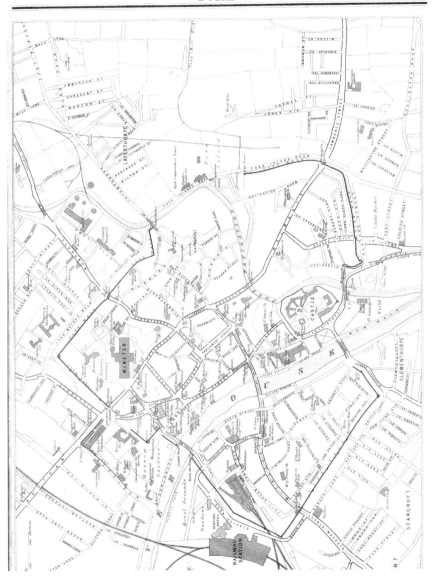

York in the 1970s

established manufacturers and traders. Some of the reason for the industrial anathema can probably be laid at the door of the Corporation whose medieval constitution, financial straits and general lack of enterprise did little to attract, promote or sustain industry or commerce at any significant level.

If the 1775 register of freemen is to be believed, only 600 enfranchised members were actually engaged in manufacturing while more were merchants, grocers or innkeepers: York it seems was now destined only to work as a parochial market town supplying its own and the surrounding area's basic needs, goods and services and those of the Church and the gentry who frequented the city. Their haunts of choice included Yorkshire House on Lendal Bridge and the Assembly Rooms round the corner in Lendal.

Communications were good by road and river and this went some way to facilitate the importation of coal – 98,000 tons annually in the 1830s – and the export of agricultural produce for example to Leeds, which, in the same period amounted to 110,000 sheep, 53,000 cattle and 30,000 tons of grain. But by the end of the century the once thriving butter trade had declined and York, though still a major ecclesiastical centre, was decidedly passé – no longer the magnet for the northern gentry it had once been and the traditional trade catering for these people suffered as a result.

The only real developments were small industries such as leather making (there were tanneries in Walmgate on the Foss and at Marygate on the Ouse) and comb and horn breaking which was active mainly around Hornpot Lane off Petergate; the comb makers worked in ivory and tortoiseshell as well as in horn. One of the more successful comb companies was Forbes and Fothergill near Toft Green; Joseph Rougier was also successful in Tanner Row – Rougier was descended from a Huguenot family of wigmakers and hairdressers; other comb makers included B. Lund in St Andrewgate. Glass was made by Prince and Prest's Fishergate Glass Works established in 1797 and flour milling was in North Street and Skeldergate; 1780 saw the establishment of Bleasdale Ltd, manufacturing and wholesale chemists behind Colliergate while other pharmaceutical and chemical manufacturers included Wright and Prest in Pavement, Edward Wallis and Son in Bedern and Thomas Bishop at North Street Postern. Breweries were being operated by the Wormald family and Thomas Hartley.

A modest amount of shipbuilding came and quickly went after the construction of six brigantines outside Skeldergate Postern for butter exports around 1770, to be followed by a further three brigantines in 1776 and three more in 1781, 1783 and 1797. Heavy industries like iron making were limited to Stodhart in Coney Street producing lamps and kitchen tools, John Spence in Bootham Bar, Masterman and Gibson in Manor Yard and Prince and Holmes on the River Foss.

The 1841 census gives us the following figures for the industries of any significance:

- glass making: fifty-four persons employed in three firms with an average workforce of eighteen persons;
- flax and linen manufacture: 118 employees in eight firms with an average of fifteen;
- iron making: twenty-five firms, six firms, average four;
- chemists and druggists: seventy-six workers in thirty-eight firms averaging two people per firm;
- 107 comb manufacturers in nine firms averaging twelve people per firm.

Coffee houses abounded in York from 1669 – there are at least thirty recorded amongst which were Parker's in Minster Yard – next to a bowling alley as shown on Horsley's 1896 map, the Garrick in Low Petergate, Wombwell and Wink's, Harrison's in Petergate and later Nessgate; Iveson's, also in Petergate, Duke's near to the Ouse Bridge; and Brigg's on the corner of Stonegate and Coffee Yard – as well as William Tuke's roasting house. As one of thirty-one York tea dealers in 1823 and importers of tea, coffee and chocolate the Tuke's were the sole holders in the north of England of a licence which permitted the processing of coffee beans and the sale of roasted coffee, tea and chocolate in the north of England. It is reasonable to assume that once drinking chocolate and cocoa became popular then, as elsewhere, they would have been added to the list of beverages available in York's coffee shops.

At the beginning of the nineteenth century the population of York (municipal borough) was 16,846; by the end of the century this had increased by over 200 per cent to 54,742 with the biggest annual increase (twenty-six per cent) coming in the 1840s soon after the arrival of the railways. Towns and cities like Leeds, Sheffield, Huddersfield, Hull and Bradford in the cauldron of the

Industrial Revolution nevertheless showed much bigger increases. But the Industrial Revolution was an event which largely passed York by; the city was strangely aloof from the 'satanic mills'. Indeed, in 1851 we can appreciate the different commercial complexions of these cities when we see that York had twice as many domestic servants in employment as the others and an above national average number of small artisan trades and shopkeepers: one shop for every fifty-five people; 2,800 people, or seventeen per cent of the city's workforce, were in service (for women the figure was seventy-five per cent) and a further ninety-one (five and a half per cent) in hospitality – hotels and inns. By comparison, manufacturing accounted for 3,170 persons, or just over nineteen per cent of the economically active. Nevertheless, at the dawn of the nineteenth century, York was England's sixteenth largest city and the fourth largest in Yorkshire after Leeds, Sheffield and Hull. By the end of the century it was the forty-first in the country and in Yorkshire, York had been surpassed by Bradford, Middlesbrough, Halifax and Huddersfield.

Before the railways many goods were transported in and out of the city on the River Ouse – one of the two arteries of the city. *White's* 1840 Directory had high hopes for the future: 'The formation of railways to open a better communication with the West of Yorkshire and the North and South of England, are in progress and with these improved modes of transit for goods, it is to be hoped that the trade of York will improve.' In the event, the railways may not have led to an expansion of the industrial base in York even though six main line rail companies were soon calling at York, but they did bring their own opportunities for employment and the obvious benefit in connectivity with the rest of the country, and indeed with the world, as access to Hull and other east coast ports was improved. Railway tracks and trains also boosted the tourism offer of the city with crowds flooding in for the races and for the Assizes to gawp at the many public executions which took place on the Knavesmire or outside the prison.

The number of people employed in York on the railways increased from forty-one in 1841 to 513 in 1851, of whom 390 came for the work from other towns in the United Kingdom. Many of these were involved in engine repair and building at the railway works where there was a 1,200 strong workforce by 1855. Carriage and wagon building followed; this all moved from Queen Street to a forty-five-acre site at Holgate and became York's first large scale industry and its biggest employer. By the end of the century there were 5,500 railway workers in the city, nearly 2,000 of whom were skilled.

Other industries in 1851 were still small fry by any comparison. The glassworks in Fishergate was ailing, and was taken over by Joseph Spence, James Meek and Thomas Spence to become the successful York Flint Glass Company; it employed 223 men turning out chemists' jars, railway lamps, beetle and wasp traps, cake shades, cruets and Daffy's Elixir glasses. The metal industry was shared between John Walker with fifty-two men, Edwin Thompson, forty-eight men, and William Knapton, eighteen men. George Steward's comb manufacturing had thirty men, while E. Steward had eighteen in the same industry; William Hebden, linen maker, had a workforce of thirty-five men, seven boys and one woman. In 1823 there were nine toy and household trinket manufacturers including John Barber of Coney Street, John Bell in Stonegate and John Jameson of College Street.

Chemicals, flour milling and printing were the only other industries of any size, with 150 chemical workers at the end of the century, ninety-eight millers, mainly at Leetham's in Wormald Cut in 1891. The number rose to 600 in 1911, while there were nearly 500 employed in the printing and publishing trade, also in 1891.

Apart from Bleasdale's in the chemical and drug making industry there was also Raimes and Company from 1818 in Micklegate and Henry Richardson and Company, fertilizer makers founded in 1824 at Skeldergate Postern in Clementhorpe. John Walker's iron foundry was very successful and received Queen Victoria's royal warrant in 1847. In 1850 they won the contract to supply the extensive railings and gates for the British Museum, and for the Sandringham Estate. In addition, much of their work was in gates and railings for the many country houses around York and at British embassies and foreign government buildings abroad, an example being the Botanical Gardens in Mauritius. The Adams Patent Sewage Lift Company Ltd was established in Peaseholme Green in 1887 to make sanitary equipment; they merged in 1919 with the 1885 iron foundry, G.W. Kirk, their biggest supplier.

Another specialist company was Thomas Cooke, an optician who went on to make sundials, microscopes and telescopes from 1837. The firm moved from

Stonegate to the Buckingham Works on Bishophill in 1856 and was run by Cooke's two sons after his death in 1868: by the end of the century they had diversified into clock making and employed 500 workers. Cooke also invented a steam car which carried fifteen passengers at a speed of fifteen miles per hour, but which was outlawed by the Road Act that prohibited vehicles travelling above four miles per hour; his sons invented the pneumatic despatch system.

The development of flour milling in York was particularly important: Henry Leetham set up his milling industry in Hungate on the banks of the River Foss in 1850, replacing his old steam mills with state of the art Hungarian steel rollers for milling the corn. In 1888 he flexed his industrial muscles by threatening to relocate to Hull if the City Corporation refused to enlarge the lock at the entry to the Foss at Castle Mills. This they duly did and grain replaced coal as the largest river cargo. At the same time very favourable terms were negotiated for the transport of Leetham's goods. Leetham went on to build his landmark five storey warehouse in 1896 on Wormald's Cut, with its nine storey castellated water tower linked to the Hungate Mill by bridges. At the time it was one of the largest mills in Europe. By then the firm had operations in Hull, Newcastle and Cardiff as well as York and was showing handsome profits of around £50,000 per year, with a wholesale customer base of around 9,000.

Chocolate city

This then was the environment in which Mary and then Henry Tuke set up their chocolate, cocoa and tea business in their Castlegate shop and in which Bayldon and Berry opened their business in St Helen's Square, and in which Mary Craven established her business in Coppergate: this was the environment in which the businesses which were eventually to become Rowntree, Terry's and Craven began their respective lives.

The confectionery trade had started to emerge as a major employer – for women as well as for men: by 1851 Joseph Terry employed 127 workers in St Helen's Square and Thomas Craven was working with 63 men and 60 boys; by the end of the century the firm employed over 200. There was also the York Confectionery Company founded in 1867 in Fossgate, then moving to

Fenwick Street off Bishopthorpe Road and specialising in candied peel and red and white mint rock for the seaside market. York Confectionery Company was owned by a man called Henderson; little is known about him apart from that he suffered from dyspnea, shortness of breath, and his factory became known as Puffy's as a result. He went bankrupt in 1909.

And then there was Lazenby & Son (York) Ltd on the Hull Road which, despite the 200 employees on its books, seems to have vanished into a York industrial history black hole. In 1915 Percy Lazenby set up as a 50:50 partner with confectioner Harold Needler in Hull; however, Needler ploughed more equity into the business and so a financially diluted Percy left and the business became part of Needler's. In 1927 Percy moved on to York where he built his own factory on the Hull Road, 'The Works', and established his own chocolate manufacturing company. Lazenby produced couverture for food and biscuit makers. Couverture is chocolate made with extra cocoa butter to give a high gloss. The company also traded under the name of Ellanson Couverture. Contracts were won with Carrs, MacFarlanes, Foxes, Huntley & Palmers and Cravens as well as supplying liquid couverture to Rowntree's.

In 1879 Rowntree's employed 100 workers; this increased to 893 in 1894 and by 1909 had reached 4,066.

Printing and publishing

Along with Oxford and Cambridge, York was for centuries one of the three premier centres of publishing in the UK. Printing came to England in 1477 with William Caxton and is first recorded in York in 1497 when Fridericus Freez, an immigrant 'docheman' is noted as 'Book Bynder' and 'Stationer' and later as a 'Buke Printer'. Hugo Goez set up in 1509 and Thomas Gent (d. 1778) published scores of chap books from Coffee Yard. During the English Civil War Charles I established his printing press in 1642, in Sir Henry Jenkins' house in St Williams' College. The royal presses rolled from March to August that year and turned out seventy-four documents including Charles' *Counsell of Warre*.

John White, Stonegate printer *'over against the Star'* (in Coffee Yard) was the only man in the country brave enough to take on the printing of William of

Orange's manifesto after his landing at Torbay in 1688. White was imprisoned at Hull for his troubles until the city surrendered to William. The king promptly rewarded him with a warrant appointing him '*Their Majesties' Printer for the City of York and the Five Northern Counties*'. His widow, Grace, was the first to establish a newspaper here in 1718, *The York Mercury*, also in Coffee Yard. She did this with Thomas Hammond, Quaker bookseller; *The York Mercury* was published first on 23 February 1719. Its title then was the pithy *The York Mercury, or a general View of the Affairs of Europe but more particularly of Great Britain, with useful observations about Trade.*

Charles Bourne took over the printing house in 1721 and in 1724 Thomas Gent, Irishman, author, publisher and printer of the local newspaper and scores of chap books acquired the business. Gent's first issue, for 16-23 November 1724, appeared under the comparatively brief new title *Original York Journal, or Weekly Courant*. By 1728 it was *The Original Mercury, York Journal, or Weekly Courant* and was published until 1739. A contemporary review described Gent's work '*for the most part below mediocrity, yet they possess a certain quaintness and eccentricity of character which are not without their charm*'. Be that as it may, Gent's books on York, Hull and Ripon are still much sought after. He had worked for printer John White, marrying into the family and inheriting the business which made him York's only typographer for a while. The four-page *York Herald and County Advertiser* was first published in 1790 in High Ousegate. It soon was making net profits of up to £1,500 and moved from weekly publication to daily in 1874, and was printed in Coney Street at the former office of the *York Courant*. In 1890 it became the *Yorkshire Herald*, and eventually increased to eight pages.

Another Quaker, William Alexander, opened a bookselling business in Castlegate in 1811, expanding into printing in 1814. Alexander refused to publish novels, considering them far too ephemeral. His self-censorship was to cost him dearly though. Walter Scott, while researching *Ivanhoe*, came to York and visited Alexander's bookshop where he suggested Alexander might publish his book. Alexander declined, saying '*I esteem your friendship but I fear thy books are too worldly for me to print*'. He paid for his rebuff, though, as the bookseller is thought to be the boring Dr Dryasdust to whom Scott

The old *Yorkshire Evening Press* barge pictured on the River Ouse outside the Coney Street offices

Printing the *Yorkshire Evening Press* in Coney Street

dedicated *Ivanhoe*. In 1796 he married Anne Tuke, daughter of William Tuke. Alexander's firm was taken over in 1865 by yet another Quaker, William Sessions, who moved the firm to Coney Street in 1894.

Ben Johnson and Co Ltd was established as a lithographic printer by Johnson and John Lancaster, specialising in railway timetables and other jobs associated with the railways. John Glaisby's bookshop and library was in Coney Street; in 1848 it had been the premises of William Hargrove's *York Herald*, next to the George Hotel and known then as Kidd's Coffee House.

Hargrove bought it from Caesar Ward, owner of the 1750-established Whig *York Courant*, in 1815; the *Courant* had been moved there from the Bagnio by Ann Ward, Caesar's widow. The magnificent statues and the bust and books have sadly gone although the publishing heritage of the building was extended when it became the offices of the then *York Evening Press* (1882) and the *Yorkshire Gazette and Herald* (which changed from a weekly in 1874 and absorbed the *Courant* in 1848). Ward was also the publisher of the first edition of Laurence Sterne's *The Life and Opinions of Tristram Shandy*. F.R. Delittle, Fine Art Printers at the Eboracum Letter Factory, 6 Railway Street later moved to Vine Street. Founded in 1888 they were publishers of the *Yorkshire Chronicle and Delittle's York Advertiser* which had a circulation of 12,000 copies in 1897. They also produced the *City Chronicle and Sheffield Advertiser;* staff numbered sixty in 1900. Books published included *Eboracum*, *The Yorkshire Road Book* and *Delittle's Picturesque York* as well as *York in 1837*. Delittle were particularly noted for the world-famous top quality wooden type used for railway posters, theatre billboards and shop window advertisements. Delittle closed in 1997 but their fame lives on in the Type Museum in London which displays a reconstruction of the Delittle type room.

York Evening Press and *York Press*

Monday 2nd October 1882 was a big news day in the city of York, for this was the day on which *The Yorkshire Evening Press* first rolled off the brand new presses at 9 Coney Street, and the people of York and round about enjoyed the first edition of their new evening newspaper, *The Yorkshire Evening Press and Herald.*

Typesetters at work at the *Yorkshire Evening Press* offices in Coney Street making up the pages

Indeed, the paper had an ambitious and extensive range, styling itself on its masthead as 'A daily newspaper for Yorkshire, Durham and adjoining counties'.

This was the paper's mission statement, as expounded in Issue 1:

"The 'Evening Press' will endeavour to give its readers the latest possible intelligence upon all subjects of interest. It will have regular correspondents in every important town in the counties through which it will circulate, and its district news will therefore be a special and interesting feature. We shall pay very special attention to all sporting events, and our commercial news will enable business men to watch the progress of the markets and the fluctuations of trade. . . Our aim is to present an epitome of everything which may occur during the day."

What awaited the news hungry readers inside the two-page broadsheet paper? A mixture of court reports, general interest and business stories, and court reports and, under the headline 'Progress in York', the following item: "We understand that Mr Win Chapman of this city has purchased a large extent of property in Leeman Road adjacent to the works of the North Eastern Railway Company and those of the York Engineering Co Ltd, and proposes erecting several hundred cottages for workmen, the rent of which will not exceed £10 a year." The paper's founder, William Wallace Hargrove, was no stranger to the commercial potential of printed media: his first headline read, "Leak And Thorp, Commerce House, York, are now showing their new designs for the autumn in Tapestry Curtains,"; jostling for front page space was the revelation that Makins & Bean of Parliament Street were now selling black and white wool at 3d an ounce. Meanwhile, in the left-hand column of that day's front page, under the heading Miscellaneous Sales, were a number of interesting items:

"Steam ploughing tackle, 'in excellent condition', FOR SALE cheap, through failing health of owner".

"For SALE, a Digitorium, as good as new. Price 5s. Excellent for strengthening and equalising the touch".

Not exactly earth shattering, but it is good local interest copy. We should of course remember that in those days the front pages of newspapers were given over to advertising. A digitorium, by the way, is a small keyboard used by pianists for exercising the fingers, without making any sound; a dumb piano in other words.

The Press building in Coney Street

Reading the news for free in Coney Street

William Hargrove was the son of Ely Hargrove, bookseller and publisher of Knaresborough. William (d. 1862) was a prominent historian and author of the invaluable *History and Description of the Ancient City of York* (1818) and the *New Guide for Strangers and Residents of the City of York* (1838). William bought the *York Herald* in 1813 and edited it until 1848 from the York City & County Library in Coney Street next to St Martin-le-Grand. William's son, Alfred Hargrove, was the author of *The Baneful Custom of Interment in Towns* which included descriptions of York's baneful cemeteries.

1954 saw the *Yorkshire Gazette* amalgamate with the *Yorkshire Herald*. On 25th June 1954 that year, the first edition of the combined *Yorkshire Herald* and *Yorkshire Gazette* was published as the *Yorkshire Gazette & Herald*. Westminster Press, owners of York and County Press, bought the *Yorkshire Evening Press* and the *Gazette & Herald* from Kemsley Newspapers in 1953.

Newspapers, of course, have changed with the times – the old school broadsheets are now themselves literally 'yesterday's papers'. *The Evening Press* is no different. The days of the shiny new presses in Coney Street are long gone when the broadsheet was painstakingly typeset by hand and printed by steam-powered presses. Today, the print edition of *The Press* is a tabloid, produced digitally with all the advantages that brings. It means that 'photographs can be flashed instantaneously around the world; stories can be filed from home or on the move from laptop computers; reports can be updated constantly throughout the day on our website; and a stream of tweets and Facebook postings keep readers up to date with the latest breaking local news'.

The Evening Press moved from Coney Street to purpose-built new offices in Walmgate in 1989 where the printing presses were housed behind the building, and newsprint was delivered by barge up the River Foss. The paper retained its name right up until the late 1990s, when it became *"The Press,"* changing from broadsheet to tabloid format on 6 September 2004, and moving to morning printing on 24 April 2006, when the title changed to reflect the new schedule. Today, the paper is printed in Bradford; those 'new' offices opened in 1989 are now student accommodation and offices; and *The Press* itself has moved into a smaller building next door – what was the old Poads corn and seed merchants building has been refurbished and new offices added behind.

Despite the relentless change, however, the aim of *The Press* – whether in print or online – remains largely the same as it was when that first edition was published 140 years ago: to 'present an epitome of everything which may occur during the day'.

Source: http://www.yorkpress.co.uk/features/features/11557526.The_Press_stays_true_to_its_founding_ideals_while_keeping_pace_in_a_digital_age/

Opening the gates of
York

YORK PEOPLE &
WHAT THEY DID

A mass busk in Coppergate in 1986.

The Saroste jugglers from Bradford entertain the crowds in April 1987.

Rudel Odermet busking in Market Street; he came all the way from Switzerland with his ten foot alphorn in August 1988. Rudel needed to keep his lip in practice during his two week holiday; he also plays the cornet and trumpet.

Stonegate busking by a Japanese visitor: his children look less than impressed; 1984.

A 1987 harmonica player in a York doorway reminding us that street entertainment was not always a barrel of laughs.

Some impressive leaping here by this Russian dancer in 1988. The etymology of 'busking' is somewhat contentious although we do know that in 1851 it was a slang word, defined variously as selling articles or obscene ballads in public houses, playing music on the streets, or performing as a sort of informal stand-up comedy act in pubs, perhaps from an earlier word meaning "to cruise as a pirate".

Harry Gration 1950–2022 – Mr Yorkshire.

St Nicholas's Field, 1989.

Outside St Lawrence's Junior School, 25 March 1966.

The Arab Legion comes to York in June 1955 for the Northern Command Tattoo – what the old lady thought of it is anyone's guess. The Tattoo was held at the Knavesmire from July 22 to August 1 that year; this photo was shot at Micklegate Bar. 1955 was the first time the traditional military event had been held in York for more than 20 years. A Bailey Bridge was constructed across the Ouse so that bandsmen could get to and from Knavesmire, and on Knavesmire itself a replica of Micklegate Bar and part of the city walls was built. Men from many different regiments – including the Arab Legion, the Household Cavalry, the Royal Corps of Signals, the Black Watch and the Durham Light Infantry – came to York for the Tattoo, with rehearsals being held several weeks beforehand. More than 100,000 people packed Knavesmire itself to enjoy the pageantry.

Arthur Robinson, secretary of the Ancient Society of York Florists with his prize-winning fuchsias. Established in 1768 the Society is the world's oldest horticultural society and runs the world's longest running flower show; it now takes place at Askham Bryan but before that was in Colliergate and at Baynes Coffee House in Petergate.

The Barbara Taylor School of Dancing in Haxby, 19 December 1992.

Napoleon first arrived in York in 1822, one year after his death on St Helena. He stood sentinel outside H. Clarke's tobacconists in Low Ousegate to whom letters were addressed simply as *'Napoleon, York'* – and would arrive. In full uniform, here he is proffering a snuff box to passers-by; Napoleon liked his snuff. He is carved out of a solid piece of oak and is the only known survivor of three made, each selling for £50. Apparently, during World War II he ended up in the River Ouse, courtesy of allied soldiers garrisoned in York; he was recovered none the worse at Naburn Lock and is now safely accommodated in the Merchant Adventurer's Hall. Another Napoleonic connection with York is the elm tree next to the water tower on Lendal bridge; this was grown from a cutting taken from an elm on Napoleon's grave on St Helena. David Handley of Whitby Street is keeping him company in 1966.

Eddie Izzard was awarded an honorary degree by York St John University in a ceremony at York Minster in 2018. The university said the honour was for his outstanding achievements as a comedian, actor, writer, fundraiser and political activist. A master of languages, he is also regularly in the headlines for his charity work, particularly his epic series of marathons which raised £2.6 million for Sport Relief.

York St John's roots go back to 1841 when the York Diocesan Training School, for teacher education, opened in May 1841 with one pupil on the register, sixteen-year-old Edward Preston Cordukes. The Students' Union building is named after him. The college changed its name to St John's College in the late 1890s, and by 1904 is was the largest Diocesan College in the country with 112 students. In 1916, half way through the Great War, the college was forced to close because all the students had gone to the front. The building was requisitioned as a military hospital until it re-opened in 1919, but the affiliated women's college in Ripon remained open, so that female students could make clothes, bandages and splints for the soldiers at the front. Ripon and York merged to become the College of Ripon & York St John in 1974. By 2001 all courses moved to the York campus and the name York St John was adopted.

May 1965 saw squatters occupying a Rowntree Mackintosh owned house at 57 Rose Street.

Girls from St Stephen's Orphanage enjoying themselves on a day trip to Filey in July 1919. The orphanage was founded in the 1870s originally in Precentor's Court, moving to Trinity Lane and then to the Mount in 1919; it closed in 1969. Its aim was to accommodate and educate poor girls who had lost one or both parents. The orphanage owned a holiday house in Filey. Image courtesy of YAYAS.

The home-made bow and arrow was *the* must have weapon. These boys were playing outside St Anthony's Hall on Aldwark. In this image from the 1940s they had probably been inspired by the swash-buckling Hollywood style of Errol Flynn as he rescued Olivia de Havilland's Maid Marian from the wicked clutches of his enemies in the *Robin Hood* film that came out just before the war.

Now, what to spend the pocket money on? – not the Park Drive cigarettes hopefully. A common scene in North Street in the 1920s as here, and into the 60s. This was a typical corner shop, selling a variety of groceries, cigarettes and confectionery. It was owned by the Hemmens family and, at this time, was run by Arthur until he was well beyond retirement age. He died in 1944. His daughter, Christiana, known to everyone as Cissie, carried on the family business into her advancing years until she called it a day in 1968 after a robbery left her traumatised. She was 98 when she died in 1984.

If we needed reminding that street life in York has not always been a bed of roses for some, then this will do the trick – homeless people in King's Square in March 1987, and one man setting off for Tadcaster.

Meet Eymund the fisherman in the Jorvik Viking exhibit. He was born about AD 948 and is faithfully reconstructed from a male skeleton unearthed in a Viking cemetery in Fishergate.

Highwayman Dick Turpin, also known as John Palmer and here played by Geoffrey Saville-Dean, enjoying a warm welcome at the Black Swan on

30 April 1971 where he was served a pint of Bass Charrington's Special Anniversary Ale. Turpin was hanged (somewhat fittingly) on the Knavesmire in 1739, for horse stealing – *'a crime worthy of death'.*

Blind Tom, the 'Inexplicable Phenomenon'. York Theatre Royal was the venue in 1853 for a concert by Miss Greenfield, a black, former slave girl; reviews in the *Yorkshire Gazette* were very favourable. In 1866 we heard that *'Blind Tom is Coming! Blind Tom, the Inexplicable Phenomenon'* who had recently wowed audiences at the St James's and Egyptian Halls in London (*York Herald*, October 20th). He too was an ex-slave and a protégé of Charles Dickens who counted him as a *'valued friend'.* At birth, poor Tom was a 'make weight' thrown into the deal when his mother was bought by a tobacco-planter: *'a lump of black flesh born blind, and with the vacant grin of idiocy'.* Notwithstanding, he turned out to be a gifted pianist and a success on the novelty and trick circuit: for example, *'his most confusing feat was to play one air with his left hand, another with his right in a different key, whilst he sang a third tune in a different key again...experts such as the Head of Music at Edinburgh testified to his accuracy'.*

The Bumper Castle was built by William Johnson, landlord of The Three Cranes in York until 1846. His widow, Elizabeth Johnson (1805-1907), took over on his death in 1879. She was the oldest licensee in the country when she died aged 102 in 1907, after 28 years behind the pumps.

Mollie (Mary) Bagot Stack founded the League of Health and Beauty, later the Fitness League, in 1930, revolutionising exercise for women. It led the way forward in setting standards for a profession then still in its infancy. Yet, she was not alone in her ideals. Rowntree's put on this display of physical training and dancing at its works on Haxby Road during the celebrations for Civic Week in June 1928, demonstrating its policy to support the growing interest in women's fitness.

Police officers learning how to deal with road accidents in 1968.

A policeman tries to buy black market tickets for an Ian Dury concert at York University. Photo courtesy of York University.

The clandestine Bar Convent community 1900. The first mass was held in April 1769 in the new Chapel, with its magnificent, but externally unobtrusive, neo-classical dome concealed beneath a pitched slate roof. Apart from the discreet dome the building has many other integral features which betray the secret nature of its activities. The chapel is situated in the centre of the building so that it cannot be seen from the street; its plain windows reveal nothing of its ecclesiastical nature and there are no fewer than eight exits, providing escape routes for the congregation in the event of a religious raid. There is also a priest's hole which can still be seen today. The nuns who still live there belong to the Congregation of Jesus which was founded by Mary Ward (1585-1645). Five nuns were tragically killed here during the 1942 Baedeker air raid.

The forty Poor Clare nuns came to York from Bruges. The first convent of the Sisters of the Second Order of Saint Francis was Plantation House in Hull Road in 1865; they moved to the obscure St Joseph's Monastery in Lawrence Street

in 1873. Until recently they lived there behind twenty-feet high walls, got up at 5am, lived in silence, were vegetarians and cultivated a six-acre garden to make themselves largely self-sufficient. The convent comprised cloisters, cells, chapel and refectory. The remaining eight Poor Clare Colettines have now moved to Askham Bryan. The image shows Sister Mary Joseph promoting the self sufficiency of the order in the 1970s by watering the winter lettuces in the walled greenhouse – 4 December 1970.

40

Poor Clare nuns 31 May 1982 – taking their first glimpse of the outside world for many years.

Camera-shy Poor Clares. 9 August 1965: a BBC film crew and the *Yorkshire Evening Press* were allowed access to the convent: the first visitors to gain entry for over 100 years.

Beer, and wine, have always been important in the economies of convents and monasteries. The Poor Clares are evidently no exception: 2 November 1991 saw Sister Mary Paul getting ready for the annual Christmas Fayre.

York Deaf and Dumb Mission members donating coal for their mission room during a coal shortage in World War I.

The Mission was founded in 1884 at a meeting in York's Guildhall and originally known as The York and District Christian Mission to the Deaf and Dumb. These sorts of Christian missions to the deaf were widespread in the late 19th century: their objective was broadly

> "the religious instruction of the Deaf and Dumb; to see as far as possible to the educational wants of Deaf-Mute children; to help the Deaf to bear patiently their daily burden; to encourage them in resisting intemperate habits; to help the needy; to find work for the unemployed; and to minister to the sick. In short to do to the Deaf and Dumb what the churches and various charitable agencies do for those who can hear and speak."

The relationship between sport and the Christian missions was strong, chiming with the Victorian idea of 'muscular Christianity'.

John Goodricke – York's deaf and dumb astronomer – was born in Groningen on 17th September 1764 and lived most of his life at the Treasurer's House; at the age of five he contracted scarlet fever which left him profoundly deaf and dumb. Notwithstanding, Goodricke became an accomplished astronomer; the plaque outside his home reads:

> 'From a window in the Treasurer's House, City of York, the young deaf and dumb astronomer John Goodrick, who was elected a fellow of the Royal Society at the age of 21, observed the periodicity of the star ALGOL and discovered the variation of CEPHEL and other stars thus laying the foundation of modern measurement of the Universe.'

He died aged 21. His cousin was Edward Piggott (1753 – 1825), another gifted York astronomer who worked with Goodricke in their observatory behind the Black Horse Inn in Bootham.

YORK PLACES – NEW, OLD AND LOST

Monk Bar undergoing repairs in 1961. Look, no scaffolding. Little Ease was a tiny prison cell inside Monk Bar, not much over five feet in diameter. In 1588 Robert Walls was imprisoned for *'drawing blood in a fray';* in 1594 Alice Bowman, a local recusant, was held here. From 1845 to 1913 a police inspector lived there, and in other rooms. It is now part of the Richard III Museum in the Bar. Built around 1330 the Bar is, at sixty-three feet, the tallest of York's Bars. Designed as a self-contained fortress, assailants had to cross each floor to reach the next flight of stairs, thus exposing themselves to defensive fire. It also features loopholes (for bows and arrows); gun ports and murder holes from which heavy objects and boiling water might be dropped. The barbican was removed in the early 1800s.

Bootham Bar road works. Bootham Bar (originally Buthum which means at the booths and signifies the markets which used to be held here) stands on the north-western gateway of the Roman fortress and was originally called Galman-lith. A door knocker was added to the Bar in 1501 for the use of 'Scotsmen' (and others presumably) seeking admission to the city. The barbican came down in 1831 and the wall steps went up in 1889. Thomas Mowbray's severed head was stuck on a pike here in 1405 for two months before it was taken down and reunited with the body. Legend has it that the head retained the freshness

of life. The Earl of Manchester bombarded the Bar in 1644 during the Civil war. The removal of the barbican was due in part to complaints by residents of Clifton: *'not fit for any female of respectability to pass through'* on account of the droppings of animals en route to the cattle market and its use as a urinal by pedestrians. The three statues on the top were carved in 1894 and feature a mediaeval mayor, a mason and a knight; the mason is holding a model of the restored Bar.

York station in 1969 looking very European.

Three more fine views of the present, third, station: this is in 1900, complete with early morning milk. York has had three railway stations. The first was a temporary wooden building on Queen Street outside the walls, opened in 1839 by the York & North Midland Railway. It was replaced in 1841, on Tanner Row within the walls, by what is now called the old York railway station and was built by Robert Stephenson on land owned by Lady Hewley's Charity almshouses.

Because through trains between London and Newcastle needed to reverse out of George Hudson's old York station in order to continue their journey, a new station, the third, was built outside the walls.

This is it in 1910; it was designed by the North Eastern Railway architects Thomas Prosser and William Peachey, which opened in 1877. It had thirteen platforms and was at that time the largest station in the world. At 800 feet long and 234 feet wide it is one of the most spectacular examples of railway architecture in the world, rightly and famously described as *'A splendid monument of extravagance'*, and *'York's propylaeum'*.

Car parking has always been a problem in York. Here are some fine motor cars parked in front of Castle Garage in Tower Street in the 1950s. The Castle Garage, which was built in the 1930s on the site of the filled-in sunken garden of Castlegate House, was demolished in 1981 to make way for a new development – a luxury 120-bedroom hotel looking out over the castle to be called The Grand Old Duke of York. This all fell through leaving York with a huge hole in the ground; today the Hilton now stands here.

More fine vehicles, this time in Exhibition Square car park in 1957.

Parking in Parliament Street in 1962.

The National Railway Museum is covered in the next four photographs. The Railway Centenary Exhibition was held in York in 1925, the success of which led to the opening of a Railway Museum in 1928, again in Queen Street. A branch of British Transport Historical Records was set up at York in 1955 to facilitate railway related research. This shows the Iron Duke being polished by Stan Knowles at the National Railway Museum in 1992. There are approximately 280 rail vehicles in the National Collection, with around 100 being at York at any one time and the remainder divided between Locomotion at Shildon and other museums and heritage railways.

Fireman Jim Fletcher and seventeen former *Mallard* drivers celebrate 30 years of the engine's 1963 retirement. LNER 4468 *Mallard* is a Class A4 4-6-2 steam locomotive built by the London & North Eastern Railway at Doncaster Works in 1938. It is the holder of the world speed record for steam locomotives at 126 mph (203 km/h). The A4 class was designed by Nigel Gresley; *Mallard* covered almost one and a half million miles (2.4 million km).

Queen Victoria getting a make-over in her train in the permanent display "Palaces on Wheels", a collection of Royal Train saloons from Queen Victoria's early trains through to those used by Queen Elizabeth II up to the 1970s.

A replica of Stephenson's Rocket. The Museum also holds a large open library and archive of railway related material; it is called Search Engine. This includes

an internationally significant collection of locomotive and rolling stock engineering drawings from railway works and independent manufacturing companies. The library holds more than 20,000 books and 800 journals, of which around 300 are active. The archive also holds a large collection of technical and test records, as well as timetables including a large number of *Bradshaw* timetables. The archives also hold some 1.75 million photographs covering the earliest era of photography to the modern day.

Layerthorpe Bridge and *The Reklaw*.
The dredger *Reklaw* ('Walker' backwards,) seen here in May 1956 was owned by J.H. Walker, builders of Layerthorpe; it plied on the Foss until its retirement in the 80s to Goole as a refurbished holiday barge for handicapped and under privileged children. The tug was owned by York Corporation.

Lendal Bridge was inspired by the need for access to the new railway and was opened in 1863 to replace the ferry which plied between the Lendal and Barker Towers. Jon Leeman was the last ferryman—he received £15 and a horse and cart in redundancy compensation. It was designed by the aptly named William Dredge. Unfortunately, his bridge collapsed during construction killing five men; it was replaced by the present bridge, designed by Thomas Page who was responsible also for Skeldergate Bridge here and Westminster Bridge in London. The remnants of Dredge's bridge were literally dredged up from the river and sold to Scarborough Council who used them in the construction of Valley Bridge.

A traffic jammed Ouse Bridge. Daniel Defoe, in his *Tour Through the Whole Island of Great Britain* described the original as *'near 70 foot in diameter; it is, without exception, the greatest in England, some say it's as large as the Rialto at Venice, though I think not.'* There were about fifty shops, a prison or kidcote, a town hall and a hospital on the bridge and from 1367 England's first public toilets are reputed to have opened here (issuing into the river): *'the place on Owsbridge callyd the pyssing howes'*. Agnes Gretehede was paid two shillings a year to keep them clean in 1544. The present Ouse Bridge was built between 1810 and 1821.

When Skeldergate Bridge used to open.

The Centurion enters York through the raised arch of Skeldergate Bridge in October 1952. Picture reproduced from a copy of *The Sphere*.

Fishergate (George Street Bar) 7 July 1961 – gateway to Selby: traffic diversions are in place while workmen restore the Bar. In Elizabethan times it was a prison for rascals and lunatics. In 1489, the bar was seriously damaged in the Yorkshire peasants' revolt against Henry VII and walled up as punishment for the locals who had rioted against a tax levied to pay for a war against Brittany; they burned the gates of the Bar after murdering the Earl of Northumberland. The gateway was not re-opened until 1834, to give better access for the cattle market. The pub you can glimpse through the Bar is 'The Phoenix': the original name until the mid 1800s was 'The Labour in Vain'. The sign depicted a white woman vigorously scrubbing a black baby in a frantic bid to make it white; her labours, of course, were in vain. The inscription read *'You may wash him and scrub him from morn till night; your labour's in vain, black will never come white'.*

Stuck in Micklegate Bar in 1969 for three hours this 20 foot lorry was carrying a load of fertilizer. One eye witness remarked 'I wouldn't mind if he was a foreigner but he's only come from Malton'.

Micklegate Bar with St Thomas's Hospital on the right with the Punch Bowl next door. Photo courtesy of YAYAS, part of the Evelyn Collection.

Bootham Bar, York: one of six exquisite Yorkshire scenes commissioned in 1934 from the studio of Charles Spindler in Alsace, France. They hang in Bettys Harrogate and Ilkley. Courtesy of Bettys & Taylors, Harrogate.

Les Acomb and Ben Nicolson grass cutting at the city walls in September 1972. It was the Backhouses who first donated the daffodils to York City Council for planting along the walls; their descendants still delight us every spring.

An unusual view of the walls.

The walls were built in the 13th and 14th century on a rampart dating from the 9th and 11th centuries. They survive for the best part of their two miles plus length, as do the four Bars and thirty-seven internal towers. Four of the six posterns and nine other towers are lost or have been rebuilt. The walls for the most part are six foot wide and thirteen foot high. They were breached in two places in the 1840s to allow access to York's second railway station and to a goods depot known as the Sack Warehouse.

In 1972 a Roman sewer was discovered below the north side of Church Street. The 52m length of the main sewer serving the Roman baths is only accessible on special open days. It was high enough to allow slaves to crawl along inside to clean it. Side channels, sluices and manhole covers are also in evidence. Analysed sewage shows the residents of York to have been riddled with worms

and bowel parasites. The discovery of spicules from marine sponges confirms what we already knew from literary evidence: that bathers used sponges as 'toilet paper' – probably for communal and not individual, personal use.

A rare black swan at the University of York lake in 1969. The black swan (Cygnus atratus) breeds mainly in the southeast and southwest regions of Australia. In western Europe, especially Britain, escapees are commonly reported. The campus lake is the largest plastic-bottomed lake in Europe and attracts many waterfowl; the campus also supports a large rabbit population, the hunting of which by students is strictly prohibited.

The famous lake again in August 1989. The first petition for a university in York was to King James I in 1617 followed by other unsuccessful attempts in the eighteenth century, one to annex it to the existing medical school.

Verger John Daly has a close look at 'Great Peter' in 1992; at 10.8 tons it is the third heaviest bell in the UK. Originally cast in 1845 it was recast in Lough-borough in 1928. The two west towers of the minster hold bells, clock chimes and a concert carillon. The north-west tower contains Great Peter and the six clock bells (the largest weighing just over 60 cwt or 3 tons). The south-west tower holds 14 bells (tenor 59 cwt or 3 tons) hung and rung for change ringing and 22 carillon bells (tenor 23 cwt or 1.2 tons) which are played from a baton keyboard in the ringing chamber – all together 35 bells.

Staff move 5,000 books (somewhat precariously) during renovation work on the Minster Library in 1980.

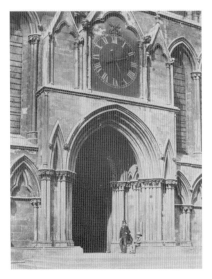

From 1750 until 1871 the south entrance to the Minster was surmounted by a splendid clock. This was installed in 1750 by Henry Hindley to replace a ramshackle mediaeval clock. Henry Hindley's Striking Clock was moved to the North Transept where it features two carved oak figures or 'Quarter Jacks' who strike the hours and quarters with their rods.

York Minster, The Deanery, and Library

The Old Palace not only housed York Minster's library and archives but also the Collections Department and the conservation studio. It is known as The Old Palace because part of the building used to be the chapel of the thirteenth century Archbishop's palace. In 1810 it was refurbished and, shortly after, the Minster's collection was installed there. The original library was the dream and ambition of King Egbert, a disciple of the Venerable Bede: he opened a school of international repute and started a collection of books. The librarianship then passed from 778-781 to Alcuin who later become one of the architects of the Carolingian Renaissance. Alcuin's catalogue featured works by many of the Church Fathers and classical authors such as Pliny, Aristotle, Cicero and Virgil – but all was tragically lost when the Minster and library were sacked by the Vikings. From 1716 to 1820, there were more than 1,200 loans by 179 different borrowers. Laurence Sterne, author of *The Life and Opinions of Tristram Shandy, Gentleman* was a regular user. By 1810 there were nearly 8,000 volumes and the library moved to its present home in Dean's Park (on the left here).

Inside St George's Baths. Zotofoam and tonic baths were installed in 1935; they were reputed to be effective against rheumatism and obesity. Cost was 2s 6d for twenty minutes. Hot air is forced into a hot bath followed by a squeeze of Zotofoam providing a body massage to *'eliminate unwanted secretions from the pores of the skin'*. Dubbed as a jacuzzi on steroids they were popular until the 1960s.

The King's Manor. This marvellous building off Exhibition Square, was originally built in 1270 as the house of the Abbott at St Mary's Abbey. It was rebuilt in 1480: the new windows providing the earliest known examples of the use of terracotta as a building material. In 1561 after the Dissolution the Lord President of the Northern Council took possession. Visitors included Henry VIII and James I; during the Siege of York in 1644 it was the Royalists' headquarters. The ornate doorway with the stunning coat of arms at the main entrance is Jacobean; the 'IR' stands for James I who ordered the Manor be converted into a royal palace for him to stay in to and from London and Edinburgh. Charles I added the royal arms, celebrating the Stuarts. After a long period of private lettings, and decay, Mr Lumley's Boarding School for Ladies occupied it from 1712-1835 and then the William Wilberforce inspired Yorkshire School for the Blind (shown here) moved in in 1833 and from the 1870s gradually restored and enlarged the buildings, adding a gymnasium and a cloister to create a second courtyard. The Blind School left in 1958; the Manor was then acquired by York City Council, who leased it to the University of York in 1963. The image shows a game of cricket among the boys and girls of the York School for the Blind taken in 1947. The ball had a rattler on it so that the players could tell where it was, and the umpire blew a whistle to communicate his decisions.

The Hospitium. This fine 14th century half-timbered building in Museum Gardens was probably designed both as a guest house for visitors to the nearby St Mary's Abbey and as a warehouse for goods unloaded from the river nearby. There was an Elizabethan knot garden with central fountain between the Hospitium and the river.

The Cold War Bunker. Opened, or rather closed, in 1961 this piece of Cold War furniture was officially No 20 Group Royal Observer HQ operated by UKWMO, the UK Warning and Monitoring Organisation. Its role was to function as one of

twenty-nine monitoring and listening posts in the event of a nuclear explosion. Decommissioned in 1991, English Heritage have opened it to the public to enable them to see the decontamination areas, living quarters, communications centre and operations rooms.

The Ice House. This brick-lined vaulted early 19th century edifice is next to the city walls near Monkgate Bar; here it is being renovated in August 1977. It was used for the storage of winter ice which, in turn, would be used for the cooling and preservation of food and drink in the summer. Contents could be kept for up to two years.

Cleaning up after the 1984 fire. They say that all things come in threes: devastating fires at York Minster are no exception. The first was in 1829 when the arsonist Jonathan Martin destroyed the Archbishop's throne, the pulpit and the choir; the second followed in 1840 when clockmaker William Groves left a candle burning and caused the south west tower to go up in flames. The York Operative Protestants Association were in session nearby and declared it a Catholic hoax. After this the Dean and Chapter, wincing no doubt at the combined £105,560 repair bills, resolved to insure the Minster. The last was in 1984: UFOs and divine retribution were ruled out and an improvident lightning strike given as the most likely cause. Whatever, the South Transept roof was destroyed and the Rose window shattered. Four years later the painstaking repairs were completed, including bosses in the South Transept vaulting designed by winners of a *Blue Peter* competition.

Barley Hall before the magnificent restoration. Parts of Barley Hall go back to 1360, when the Hall was built as the York town house for Nostell Priory, the Augustinian monastery near Wakefield, by Thomas de Dereford, the Prior from 1337 to 1372. The Priors of Nostell were prebendary canons of York Minster and attended ceremonies, services and business meetings in the city; a hostel, therefore, made good commercial sense. However, by the 15th century, the Priory had fallen on hard times and Barley Hall was leased out to private tenants. By the 17th century it was subdivided into a number of smaller dwellings so that the 'screens passage' – the internal corridor area at the end of the Great Hall – came to be used as a public short-cut through from Stonegate to Swinegate. To this day it remains a public right-of-way, known as Coffee Yard. By Victorian times, the house was 'a warren of tradesmen's workshops' and its last use before being sold for redevelopment in 1984 was as a plumber's workshop and showroom. The Hall was painstakingly restored to its former glory and it re-opened to the public in 1993. Barley Hall is named after Professor Maurice Barley, founder president of York Archaeological Trust.

St William's College complete with rendering covering the famous beams. Originally the house of the Prior of Hexham it is named after Archbishop William Fitzherbert (St William) and built in 1465 by order of Warwick the Kingmaker. From about 1890 the 15th century half timbering was covered in stucco; it was removed again in 1906. The college was split into tenements at the time but formerly was home to the Minster's Chantry: twenty-three priests and their provost. The priests, in Bedern, had been indulging in '*colourful nocturnal habits*' and were re-billeted in the nearby college so that their behaviour could be monitored more closely. One incident involved one of the cathedral freelances hitting a man over the head with the blunt end of an axe. Charles I established his propaganda Royal

YORK. ST. WILLIAMS COLLEGE.

printing house here during the Civil War and it was used as the Royal Mint at one time. The central doors were made by Robert Thompson of Kilburn: his trademark mouse can be seen on the right-hand door.

Inside the college.

The Assembly Rooms, November 1991 with architect David Green contemplating the options and opportunities for his makeover. One of the earliest neo-classical buildings in Europe, situated in Blake Street, the 1732 Assembly Rooms were designed by the Earl of Burlington in the Palladian style; they were paid for by subscription to provide the local gentry with somewhere sumptuous to play dice and cards, dance and drink tea, as featured in Smollett's *The Expedition of Humphrey Clinker*. The building epitomised the age of elegance and helped make York the capital of north country fashion – a northern Bath. The main hall is surrounded by forty-eight magnificent Corinthian pillars. Sedan chair men met in the cellars here; it was requisitioned by the Food Office in 1939. In 1751 the seats from the aisles were removed to the front of the columns for use by ladies with wide hooped skirts, too wide for them to pass between the columns, as pointed out by the Duchess of Marlborough.

The beautifully restored Assembly Rooms – now an Italian restaurant. One early 1960s Assembly Room lunch involved 380 vegetarian meals, including food for ten vegans – all very new then. Hunt balls and army functions for officers and

ASSEMBLY ROOMS, YORK, MAIN HALL

wives from Catterick were frequent and at one Tadcaster Hunt Ball the guests reputedly included Christine Keeler, Mandy Rice Davies and John Profumo.

Clifford's Tower from the pillars of York Crown Court. The York Courthouse was built in the 1770s and is the original site of the York County Assizes. In 1971 the York Assizes was replaced by the York Crown Court. Clifford's Tower was originally King's Tower, or even the 'Minced Pie', but from 1596 is named after Francis Clifford, Earl of Cumberland, who restored it for use as a garrison after it had been partly dismantled by Robert Redhead in 1592. An alternative

etymology comes from Roger de Clifford whose body was hung there in chains in 1322. Built in wood by William the Conqueror when he visited to establish his northern headquarters in 1190, the tower was burnt down when 150 terrified York Jews sought sanctuary here from an antisemitic mob; faced with the choice of being killed or forced baptism, many committed suicide; 150 others were slaughtered.

THE STREETS
OF YORK

An unusual view of Coney Street. The earliest record of the name is in 1213 when it was called Cuningstreta, from the Viking word konungra for king and straet – street. Later writers refer to it as Cunny Street. So, it was, and is, King's street. The fine clock outside St Martin Le Grand church dates from 1668; the admiral – perhaps enjoying a promotion – stands on the 1778 clock with his sextant, fixing his position by the sun. He was bombed to the ground during the 1942 Baedeker Raid but luckily found by Eric Milner White, Dean of York, and kept until the restoration of the clock in 1966.

Alf Palmer, caretaker of St Martin le Grand, inspects the Admiral's Clock, after its hands froze during a bitter night early in 1969.

A rooftop view in 1942, checking Coney Street roofs after the Baedeker Raid; opposite is the Flying Services Club HQ.

Goodramgate in 1893. The street was named after Guthrum, a Danish chief active around 878. Sanderson's Temperance Hotel can be seen on the right. The York Temperance Society was set up in 1830 with forty subscribers and Joseph Rowntree as Secretary; membership grew to nearly 1,000 by 1936 – 3.3 % of the city population at this time. In 1929 there were three other temperance hotels in York: *The Minster Commercial* in St Martin's Crescent off Micklegate; *Frank's* at 134 Micklegate and *Young's Private & Commercial* at 24 High Petergate.

The Grade I listed Lady Row cottages (numbers 60-72) date from 1316. They are the oldest surviving jettied cottages in Britain. Originally nine or ten houses for the priests at neighbouring Holy Trinity church, the one at the southern end was demolished in 1766 to make way for a gateway to the 13th-15th century Holy Trinity church (near left). They each comprised one room ten by fifteen feet on each floor. Rents collected went to pay for chantries to the blessed Virgin Mary in nearby churches. Two pubs occupied the cottages at various times: *The Hawk's Crest* from 1796-1819 and *The Noah's Ark* around 1878.

King's Staith with the King's Arms in the centre – an early 17th century building on King's Staith, traditionally a hotbed of crime and prostitution. Originally the pub had no fireplaces or room partitions so it may have been a custom house, or a warehouse. Very thick walls protect it from floods which recur to this day with alarming regularity. Due to the flooding, the cellars are on the first floor. Bodies of criminals were laid out here before being hung on and then flung from old Ouse Bridge just along the staith.

It was first recorded as a pub in 1783 or 1795 as the Kings Head; then in the 19th century licensee George Duckitt renamed it as 'Ouse Bridge Inn'. It reverted to its old name in 1974.

A busy Queen's Staith with boats jostling with each other to load and unload.

Jubbergate. Note the boy on the right with his stilts. Originally the street was named Joubrettagate – the street of the Bretons in the Jewish Quarter – and Jubretgate. Over the years occupants have included Webster's kitchen and bath-ware shop which became Pawson's, specialists in rubber-ware; *The White Rose Inn* which became Forrington's furnishers around 1920: at one stage in its life it was home to six families. Jubbergate originally extended to cover what is today Market Street as far as Coney Street. York's first police station was here until 1880 when it moved to Clifford Street.

During the 1830s, the Festival Concert Rooms were built at the rear of the Assembly Rooms as the number of arts and learned societies in the city increased. The buildings between the concert rooms and Finkle Street are said to have been removed in 1859-62 when the street was widened under the provisions of the Lendal Bridge Act. It seems likely that the buildings later to be known as Museum Chambers and Museum Street Rooms and regarded as part of the Festival Concert Rooms were erected at this time, as were the adjoining Thomas's Hotel and the Board of Guardians' offices. The concert room frontage to Museum Street had certainly been completed by 1889.

Museum Street – the buildings on the right have been demolished and replaced with the car park.

The last word in civic pride in the Shambles? Woman scrubbing down the street.

Christmas 1963 in the Shambles.

At the junction of King's Court and Newgate, Pump Court (or Yard) was the site of one of the many water pumps and wells that served the city. Piped water was turned on in parts of the city between 1677 and 1685; a public bathhouse opened in 1691. John Wesley preached in a room (the 'Oven') here in 1753 (one of twenty-six visits to the city); it became an official place of worship for Methodists in 1754. One of the country's only two surviving lantern tower windows is in Pump Court, tragically, almost hidden from public view. Betty Petre lived here; she kept her cattle in the court before slaughter in Shambles; Herr Huber collected sheeps' guts and washed them in a drain before exporting them to Germany to make fiddle strings. Other residents included a chimney sweep and a prostitute, referred to locally as *'an old knock'*.

George Hudson Street or Station Street? The mercurial Mr Hudson fell out of favour in York when his financing of the local railways became the subject of a number of enquiries. York has been a major railway centre since 1839 when the first trains came and went from the city. Its future as a hub was allegedly ensured when Hudson – the 'Railway King' – convinced a compliant George Stephenson, apparently, to *"mak all t'railways cum t' York"*.

Stephenson's decision had a huge impact on the city, boosting it socially, culturally, commercially and industrially; an impact which has resonated in York and the surrounding region for some 150 years and still resounds today.

A superb Hayes postcard showing a buzzing Micklegate. Micklegate Bar was originally called Mickleith which means great gate; the royal arms are those of Edward III; the arch is Norman, the rest 14th Century, the side arch was added in 1753. Being on the road to and from London this was the Bar through which royal visitors entered York. Edward IV, Richard III, Henry VII, Margaret Tudor,

James I, Charles I (on three Civil War occasions) and James II all passed through. A truculent Henry VIII was scheduled to enter here but, in the event, came in through Walmgate Bar. Heads and quarters of traitors were routinely displayed on the top, most famously: Lord Scrope of Mastan in 1415; Sir Henry Percy (Hotspur) after his part in the rebellion against Elizabeth I; Richard Duke of York after the Battle of Wakefield in 1460, prompting Shakespeare to write: *"Off with his head and set it on York's gates; so York did overlook the town of York"* (Queen Margaret in *Henry VI);* Thomas Percy in 1569 – his head remained there for two years. Removal of heads without permission was, not inappropriately, punishable by beheading – guess where the heads ended up. The last displays were in 1746 after the Jacobite Rebellion at Culloden. The barbican was removed in 1826 to allow a circus access to the city; the east side arch was built in 1827.

Micklegate Bar. The Bar Convent on the right down from St Thomas's Hospital was demolished in 1862. In 1851 it was an almshouse 'for aged widows' taking in permanent residents and travellers for food and lodging. Until 1791 these widows had to beg on the streets for four days every year to qualify for their alms. Next door is Howard's Punch Bowl. A later Punch Bowl stands on the site now, indicative, like the pub of the same name in Stonegate, of the vogue for drinking punch from the end of the seventeenth century. As a new, fashionable drink symbolizing change it caught on amongst the Whigs, leading to the sign of the punchbowl denoting inns patronised by Whigs. The conservative Tories stuck with their sack, claret and canary. Chapman, the bookseller and stationer, is on the left.

Pavement showing the late lamented St Crux.

One of the most heinous acts of Victorian civic vandalism to be visited on a city was the dynamiting of the cupola-topped St Crux in 1887 on health and safety grounds. More happily, some of the church's treasures can be seen in the Parish Hall which was built from the rubble, not least the beautiful 1610 monuments to Sir Robert and Lady Margaret Watter. Watter was Lord Mayor of York in 1591 and 1603; he bestowed his gold chain of office on the city: *'conteyninge in weight xxtie ounce lack half a quarter or ther aboute'* – it has been worn by every York Mayor since. Sir Robert gave James VI of Scotland breakfast on his march south.

Pavement is called thus because around 1329 it was the only clear piece of paved land in the centre of the city. Paving was unusual then. Before that it was called Marketshire and was the site of markets (there once was a market cross here), proclamations and public punishments in days when the punishment was made, and seen, to fit the crime: for example, drunks were made to stand on barrels with pint pots on their heads and goose thieves were put in the stocks with goose wings draped unceremoniously around their necks. Catholic Thomas Percy, Earl of Northumberland, was executed here in 1572 for his opposition to Elizabeth I. The fine Market Cross was demolished in 1813 to make room for more market stalls; another fine Market Cross in Saturday Market was similarly destroyed.

A wonderfully atmospheric photo of Davygate; this shows the Davy Hall restaurant about 1929, and a superb vintage car waiting outside.

Davygate is named after David le Lardiner (clerk of the kitchen). His job was to stock the King's larder; in the 12th century David's father, John, was the Royal lardiner for the Forest of Galtres – a title which became hereditary – David received land from King Stephen in 1135. Davygate was also the site of the local forest courthouse prison – the only one in the land for incarcerating transgressors of forest laws.

Spurriergate was home to J. Backhouse & Son Ltd, Nurserymen (pictured here in 1924) – an early day, state-of-the-art garden centre run by Darlington Quaker James Backhouse originally in Fishergate with 'branches' in Acomb, Poppleton

Road and Toft Green. The three shops here were demolished to make way for Woolworth's. The Backhouse brothers bought the gardens of George Telford, another celebrated gardener who, according to Francis Drake in *Eboracum* was 'one of the first that brought our northern gentry into the method of planting all kinds of forest trees, for use and ornament'. James and his brother Thomas were nationally celebrated nurserymen: their gardens were collectively called the *Kew of the North*. They were responsible for the cultivation of numerous rare plants, some of which James brought back from South Africa and Australasia. A particularly striking feature was a twenty-five feet high Alpine gorge built with 400 tons of rock – a spectacle which led to a surge in rockeries all over the country. In 1938 the nurseries were sold to the Corporation who made them into a park; this lasted until 1946 when it was all covered over. Backhouse had been producing catalogues long before 1821 when the second edition of their pithily titled *Catalogue of Fruit & Forest Trees, Evergreen & Deciduous Shrubs, Ornamental Annual, Biennial Plants, also of Culinary, Officinal & Agricultural Plants* was published.

St Helen's Square – before Bettys took over the corner on the right. Their neo-Georgian building in was fitted out in 1937. The story of Bettys begins in September 1907 when a twenty-two-year-old Fritz Butzer arrived in England from Switzerland with no English and less of an idea of how to reach a town that sounded vaguely like 'Bratwurst', where a job awaited him. Fritz eventually landed up in Bradford and found work with a Swiss confectioners called Bonnet & Sons at 44 Darley Street. Cashing in on the vogue for all things French, Fritz changed his name to Frederick Belmont; he opened his first business in July 1919 – a cafe in Cambridge Crescent, Harrogate, on three floors fitted out to the highest standards. In 1936 Frederick travelled on the maiden voyage of *The Queen Mary*. He was so impressed that he commissioned the ship's designers to turn what had been an old furniture shop in York into his most sophisticated tea rooms – and that is what you still get in the art deco upstairs function room.

Poverty in Walmgate: Walmgate, like Hungate, was a place notorious for its great poverty, crime, alcohol-related violence and prostitution for many years. The infant mortality rate was one in three before age one – as highlighted by Seebohm Rowntree's ground-breaking *Poverty: A Study in Town Life* in 1901 for which researchers visited 11,500 families and found that twenty-five per cent of the city population was visibly poor – in *'obvious want and squalor'*. The pungent smell of hide, skins and fat from local industries added to the horror of the place. At the end of the 1880s there were 8,000 midden privies in York, many here and in Hungate. In Walmgate in 1913, the death rate was twenty-three per 1,000, almost twice York's average. Using powers under the

1930 Housing Act, York Corporation began to clear the slums: streets off Walmgate and in Hungate were demolished, and residents moved to new estates outside the city centre.

Hungate poverty. Hungate derives from Hundgate – street of the dogs – a common Viking street name. As a result of explosive findings in Seebohm Rowntree's *Poverty*, and 1914 York's med-

ical officer, Edmund Smith, produced reports condemning streets in Hungate and Walmgate as unfit for habitation; '*The back yards in Hope Street and Albert Street and in some other quarters can only be viewed with repulsion – they are so small and fetid, and so hemmed-in by surrounding houses and other buildings... There are no amenities; it is an absolute slum.*' At the 1921 census York's population was 84,052 with 18,608 inhabited houses (equivalent to 4.5 persons per dwelling). Despite this abject poverty and the flooding, these Wrays Yard residents in Hungate can still smile back at us.

Washing day (probably Monday) at Nos 5 and 6 Hill's Yard in c1933. The yard opened out off Navigation Road and into Walmgate. The yard was also known as Marston's Yard. Note the mangle in the foreground.

This photograph from 1984 shows the bridge over the A19 at St Peter's crumpled into the street. According to the caption, it had been 'destroyed' by a lorry carrying an earth digger, which tried to drive under it – only to find the bridge wasn't quite as high as the driver had thought. Founded by St Paulinus of York

in AD 627 as St Peter's Grammar School along with the Minster Song School close to where York Minster now stands. St Peter's is one of the oldest schools in the world, Chengdu Shishi High School China (143 BC) and Jondi Shapour in Gundeshapur, Persia (AD 271) are the oldest; it is the third oldest school in England, after The King's School, Canterbury (597) and Rochester.

November 1, 1980: A 100-year-old train carriage is lowered into the garden of railway enthusiast John Rathmell's house in Melton Avenue, Clifton.

Two contrasting shots of Thomes Herbert's House and the Golden Fleece pub in Pavement; the latter is from 1988 when the half timbering had been exposed again. The ancient *Golden Fleece* still survives (with its impressive golden sheep hanging above the door) – as does the 15th century timber framed Tudor mansion once the home of Thomas Herbert, Bart. born there in 1606. Coning's the grocers is to the right – before that Rowntree's shop.

PUBS, HOTELS & CAFÉS

This, York's smallest pub, and one of the best, was opened in 1798 when the back of the pub faced on to Fossgate and the front was in Lady Peckett's Yard. It was one of two local Blue Bells – the other was in Walmgate. In 1845 it was the meeting place of the Chartist Cooperative Land Society, an ill- conceived organisation which urged working class people to become self-sufficient, spurning factory for field.

In 1976. The Quaker, largely teetotal, Rowntrees were responsible for physically turning the pub around in 1903, no doubt because one of their temperance-preaching Adult schools happened to be in Lady Peckett's Yard right behind the pub. It is York's only Grade II* Listed Edwardian décor pub with that unaltered 1903 interior. The Blue Bell hosted fund raising meetings to raise the £2,000 needed to buy land for a ground at Fulfordgate (Eastwood Avenue) for the nascent York City and, later, York City FC held their board meetings here; in World War II it served as a soup kitchen. Women were barred from the public bar until as recently as the 1990s.

In 1972. Since 1903, the licence has changed hands only six times. George Robinson, founding director of York City FC, took over that year. When he died in 1948, the licence passed to his wife Annie. When she passed away in 1963, their daughter Edith Pinder took over, and she remained until retiring in 1991.

Football fans in The Spread Eagle in Walmgate, in 1997

York's NAAFI

More new technology, at the NAAFI in 1996.

Horse drawn tramcar on the point of departure for York from the Plough Inn, Fulford in June 1905. The building is at least 300 years old; records show it serving as The Plough Inn as early as 1822. Before that it was a coach house. Bermaline bread was produced by the bakers Montgomery and Company, who were based at Gimmersmill in Haddington, Scotland. The company owned the mill and produced this famous bread between 1897 and 1970. The loaf was made from wheaten malt which changed the starch content into dextrin and malt sugar, yielding abundant nutrition and energy. They advertised it as "The Golden Bread For Glowing Health, Ask Your Baker For Bermaline."

Rock Café, outside…

…and inside, sometime in 1998 in Micklegate.

The Kavern Club in 1964, also in Micklegate.

The Kavern Club started life as a coffee bar; it was in the basement of the Labour Party headquarters, and decorated with grafitti. By 1964 there were a hundred or so local groups performing in York: allegedly the crime rate fell because most young people were either performing in groups or watching them.

A good, if a little overcrowded, day out beckons outside the Black Swan in 1910, courtesy of H. Lawson, 'pioneers of motor excursions'. The upstairs room here was the venue for illegal cockfights; the grill used by the guard to watch the stairs can still be seen. It is first recorded as a pub, the Swan, in 1787. In 1808 a Mrs Weston hit the headlines when she gave birth to a baby boy in the pub. Mrs Weston proudly showed her son around the city in the light of the press interest: 'extraordinary diminutive of the human species, though without deformity, being but 34 inches high'. General Wolfe's family lived here; as the sign to the left indicates, it was the headquarters of the York Layerthorpe Cycling Club from 1834. The Leeds Arms (closed 1935) was next door on the corner of Haymarket; the Woolpack was over the road.

Bettys. Musical entertainment 31 August 1979: 'The quiet elegance of The Palm Court Hotel is being recreated at a restaurant in York'.

A typically busy day at Bettys 10 September 1988. Not that much has changed.

The much missed Blake Head Bookshop & (Vegetarian) Café in Micklegate in 1992.

Priory Street Centre Nursery taking over the Blake Head in 1996. Some impressive artworks there.

The Maltings when it was The Lendal Bridge Inn. This wonderful pub was originally called the Railway Tavern (because it was near York's two railway stations), and later The Lendal Bridge Inn (because it is just off the bridge); it was established in 1842. At the time the photo was taken, the owner purchased the pub from Bass in 1992, and renamed it The Maltings. It is next door to what was Botterill's Repository for Horses, built in 1884 and reduced in height by a half in 1965 when it became a car dealership. Patrick Nuttgens described the original building as *an exotic red and yellow Byzantine building with ramps inside, up which the horses were led to their stalls – a kind of multi-story horse car park*. It was frequently used by patrons of the 1868 Yorkshire Club for gentlemen (River House) in from the country, just over Lendal Bridge. The advert for Hunt's Ales reminds us that York's biggest brewery was the Ebor Brewery founded by Joseph Hunt in 1834; he was registered as a hop and seed merchant at 2 Monk Bar. By 1851 he was Brewer, Malster, Hop, Seed & Guavo Merchant at 20 Aldwark. Their Ebor Brewery was established in 1895 and in 1904 took over Robert Brogden, Sons Co along with their sixty or so licensed pubs. Ebor was acquired by Cameron & Co of West Hartlepool in 1954.

YORK EVENTS

On 15 September 1971, 160 Gurkha bandsmen marched through the city into St Helen's Square. In 2015 the Gurkha Signal Regiment who are stationed at Imphal Barracks were awarded the freedom of the city.

Four scenes from the 1954 York Festival. There were three York Festivals of the Arts: the first in 1951 as a hugely successful satellite event in the Festival of Britain. The Director of York City Art Gallery, Hans Hess, remarked that 'York found its soul'. The others took place in 1954 and 1957. The undisputed star of the festivals were performances of the *York Mystery Plays*, dramatically and atmospherically set in the ruins of St. Mary's Abbey. It was not until 1954 that a wagon play, *The Flood,* toured the streets.

Actors of the calibre of Mary Ure, Judi Dench and Christopher Timothy cut their teeth here. The brilliant, inspirational Hans Hess was curator at the York City Art Gallery from 1947 until 1954 when he took over as York Festival Director, the second only in reputation to the Edinburgh Festival.

Angry looking Viking with police escort at the 1986 Jorvik Viking Festival.

Viking boats enthral the crowds on King's Staith at the 1985 festival.

The Yorkshire Air Museum is the largest independent air museum in Britain and is also the location of The Allied Air Forces Memorial. It is located at the former World War II RAF Bomber Command Station at Elvington. It was also the only base used by the French heavy bomber squadrons during the war and today features over sixty historic aircraft and vehicles. Russell Richardson in July 1982 at Elvington Air Museum, swivelling the turret of a Lancaster bomber.

Handley Page Victor K2, XL231 'Lusty Linda' at Elvington stood on the runway. Although operational and in working order the aircraft is permitted only to perform fast taxis and is not cleared for take offs. She is still in her desert colours from the first Gulf War which was her last active campaign. 'Lusty Linda' was used in its later days as a mid-air refuelling tanker.

A flypast by a Shackleton in 1991.

Before 1951 when Harrogate became the official home, the Great Yorkshire Show was held in a different town every year. It came into being in October 1837 when a group of leading agriculturalists, led by the third Earl Spencer, met at the Black Swan Hotel in Coney Street, York to discuss the future of the farming industry. The result was the inauguration of the Yorkshire Agricultural Society – whose aims were to improve and develop agriculture and to hold a prestigious annual show. The first Yorkshire Show was held in Fulford, York, in 1838. The first recorded attendance figures were in 1842 when the Show was again held in York attracting 6,044 visitors. At the *Yorkshire Gazette* tent, this group of well-dressed gentlemen included Alfred Humphries (1869-1952), head gardener at Backhouse Nursery in Acomb. I'm struggling with how the *Yorkshire Gazette* offer of 'Free Insurance' would be of any use to you if you did suffer a fatal accident.

Bathing *au naturel* in Yearsely Swimming Pool – the swimming pool here was simply a stretch of the River Foss where the river bed was concreted over. The tendency for young boys to swim naked there deterred most females. The City of York benefitted from Joseph Rowntree's sense of civic responsibility and philanthropy when in 1909 the Yearsley Road swimming baths opposite his Haxby Road factory were gifted to the people of York.

Will you ever find your car again after the last race? Horse races have been run at York since the reign of Roman Emperor Septimius Severus. In 1607, racing is known to have taken place on the frozen River Ouse, between Micklegate Tower and Skeldergate Postern. The first records of a race meeting are from 1709, when efforts were made to improve the flood-prone course at Clifton Ings; all to no avail, so in 1730 racing moved to Knavesmire, where today's course remains. York architect, John Carr, designed and built the first Grandstand in 1754.

Crowds at York races during the Ebor Meeting, 17 August 1972. Old weighing scales at the Racecourse Museum.

Mr O.S. Eccles is the thatcher repairing and extending the stewards' box, 20 August 1955.

Improving the drainage at York City's Bootham Crescent.

York City FC ground staff clearing the snow from the terraces for the FA Cup 1st round game against Morecambe 7 December 1968; York won 2-0.

Some of the 28,123 crowd at the York City v Huddersfield

Town match in the March 1938 5th round FA Cup tie at Bootham Crescent. It was a record crowd for the club; capacity was 7,872. The game finished goalless, with Huddersfield winning the Leeds Road replay 2-1 in front of 58,066 and going all the way to Wembley, where they lost 1-0 after extra time to Preston North End.

YORK BUSINESS & INDUSTRY

York, because of its cloth trade and the ancillary industries associated with it in the 14th century, was described as '*the foremost industrial town in the North of England.*' In 1384 there were 800 weavers in the city. This prosperity was short-lived though, and the trade in cloth declined to such a degree that, as we have seen, a visitor to the city in the seventeenth century, Thomas Fuller, remarked: '*the foreign trade is like their river...low and flat.*'. The railway and confectionery industries were soon to change York's industrial landscape.

Craven's of York

The Coppergate factory in 1965. The confectionery giant was in Coppergate until the 1950s, when it moved to Poppleton. The company originated in

1803 when Joseph Hick set up as a twenty-nine-year-old in York as Kilner and Hick, confectioners. Kilner left town leaving Hick with the business which he relocated to 47 Coney Street next door to what was then the Leopard Inn, opposite St Martin le Grand.

Mary Ann Hick was born in 1829 and in 1851 she married Thomas Craven who had served an apprenticeship with George Berry, later a partner at Terry's; he bought a building in Pavement from William Dove and a further site at 10 Coppergate, both of which expanded his own confectionery business. In 1860 Joseph Hick died and his estate was divided up between his three children.

In 1862 Mary Ann's husband died leaving her with three young children to raise and two businesses to run. Near to starvation she took up the challenge, amalgamated the businesses, changed the name of the company to M.A. Craven, and ran it until her death in 1902. In 1881 her son, Joseph William, had joined the firm. There were four Craven's retail shops in the city, one of which, Craven's Mary Ann Sweet Shop, was in the Shambles and featured a sweet museum on the first floor where visitors could see 150 years of the 'Art, Trade, Mystery and Business of the Confectioner'. Today the Craven brand is owned by Tangerine Confectionery which manufacturers sugar confectionery from their plant in Low Poppleton Lane.

Luxury lines in an early Terry trade catalogue.

Redfearn National Glass Company

Bottles, bottles everywhere in 1977. York's first glassworks was opened in 1794 by Hampston and Prince near Fishergate making flint glass and medicinal phials. The York Flint Glass Company was set up in 1835 and by 1851

was a bigger employer than either Terry or Craven. In 1930 it was incorporated as National Glass Works (York) Ltd which became Redfearn National Glass Company in 1967; demolished in 1988 it is replaced by the Novotel. Sand for the works came via the Foss Islands Branch Line; the line (operational from 1879 to 1988) also served the electricity power station and cattle market.

Terry's of York

Demolition of the Clementhorpe buildings in 1987.

Eating the profits in 1979.

Terry's iconic clock face – from the inside – during redevelopment of the factory. Courtesy of tassadar@ midlandsheritageforum.co.uk

Picking chocolates for chocolate boxes in 1991.

Terry's in St Helen's Square.

Terry's after the wrecking ball.

Adams Hydraulics

1990 at the furnace.

The company was based at Peasholme Green for more than 100 years until 1990, when it moved to Clifton Moor, where it remains today. It was founded by Samuel Henry Adams in 1885 and was originally called Adams of York and London. The name was then changed to Adams Hydraulics Ltd in 1903. The company specialises in the manufacture and supply of apparatus and plant for sewerage and sewage purification.

T. Cooke & Sons

Wartime work at Cooke, Troughton & Simms. Over 3000 men and women of York keep the war effort on target making gun sights, telescopes and tank periscopes. Some 3,300 employees poured into the factory every day, including 1,400 women.

Thomas Cooke came to York in 1829 and made his first telescope using the base of a whisky glass for a lens and a tin for the tube. In 1837 he opened his first instrument-making shop at 50 Stonegate with a loan of £100 from his wife's uncle. Cooke quickly gained a reputation for high quality and was soon making microscopes, opera glasses, spectacles, electrical machines, barometers, thermometers, globes, sundials and mathematical instruments as well as telescopes. By 1844 he had expanded and moved to 12 Coney Street. In 1866 Thomas Cooke branched out into three-wheeled steam cars which reached the dizzy speed of fifteen mph; they, were, however, outlawed by the Road Act which prohibited vehicles travelling in excess of four mph. In those days a man with a red flag had to walk in front of any vehicle not pulled by a horse. Cooke fitted his steam engine into a boat and travelled on the Ouse, free of horses and red flags. He died in 1868. In 1914 a new factory was built on Bishophill, York, to meet the demand for war work. Cooke Troughton & Simms became a subsidiary of Vickers in 1924. Their Haxby Road factory was built in 1938, and the works continued making theodolites, microscopes and other optical tools into the 1980s. Bio-Rad took over in 1990s.

York Gas Light Company travelling showroom. Gas lighting, or '*the lamp that wouldn't blow out*', was introduced to York by the York Gas Light Company in 1823 on the banks of the River Foss near Monk Bridge. In 1836 the York Union Gas Light Company was formed; rivalry was intense with workmen from the former going round slyly filling in the latter's excavations; the two companies eventually amalgamated in 1843 to form the York United Gas Light Company. In 1824 there were 250 consumers; this had risen to 34,000 by 1963. In 1912 coverage was extended to seven miles from the Ouse Bridge to take in Haxby, Wigginton and Strensall.

The former gas works at Heworth Green in 1978 sharing the skyline with York Minster.

Ben Johnson's & RR Donnelley. Ben Johnson's printworks was founded in 1880. Its works in Boroughbridge Road, York, opened in 1934; the printing presses kept rolling for the next six decades. Here we see the first telephone directories under a new 10-year contract leave the site in 1982.

It is 95 years this year since the Second Anglo-Scottish Beet Sugar Corporation opened the factory in Poppleton in 1926. Here is the York sugar beet factory in 1982. The factory opened to process sugar beet farmed around York. By

1930 it was handling 133,000 tons of beet a year. During the war, sugar was classified as an 'essential element' of Britain's wartime food production, and skilled sugar workers were accorded 'reserved occupation' status.

Anyone who lived in or near York will know the sweet smell that was carried in all that steam.

Children play near Clifton Bridge, in the shadow of the factory in 2006.

The factory with its landmark chimney, pictured over a flooded ings, in its last 'campaign' at the end of the 2006/2007 harvest. The effects of the closure were felt far beyond the factory gates, not least among the 1,200 or so farmers around the region who supplied the factory with beet.

Rowntree's

Pavement from Parliament Street showing the Rowntree grocery shop, in 1944, rebadged as T. Coning & Sons – the company which bought the shop when Joseph Rowntree sold the business to focus on cocoa and chocolate production at the Tanner's Moat factory. The Rowntree name remained prominent on the façade for many years after the sale to Coning; a sure indication that the Rowntree name was synonymous with quality and was well worth cashing in on.

Henry Coning in 1928.

The elder Joseph Rowntree came to York from Scarborough where his father ran a grocer's shop and where Joseph had worked since he was eleven. Joseph too became a grocer with a shop in Pavement; its apprentices included George Cadbury. He bought the Pavement shop in 1822 on his twenty-first birthday, at an auction at *The Elephant & Castle Inn* in Skeldergate; the auctioneer was so drunk that Joseph and his friend, James Backhouse, had to plunge his head in a sobering barrel of cold water so that the sale could proceed.

Workmen replacing brickwork in the huge Elect Cocoa sign at the Haxby Road Rowntree factory in 1983. 1880 saw the production and launch in 1880

of cocoa essence – *Rowntrees Elect*, *'more than a drink, a food'*, made from top quality cocoa. The name 'Elect' came from the apothecary trade where it was used to signify an efficacious drug. *Elect* was *'an extremely light powder, the essential product of the cocoa bean after it had been roasted and ground and the fat (cocoa butter) taken out by hydraulic pressure.'*

Rowntree Mackintosh bricklayer Ron Ellis knocks out the bricks which formed the Rowntree's Cocoa sign, in 1982.

High level exterior decorating at the Rowntree factory.

A solemn looking company meeting in the 1920s. Note the women's hair styles. In April 1914 'the very dangerous practice of wearing unprotected hat-pins' had been highlighted in Rowntree's staff magazine, *Cocoa Works Magazine*: 'in January during the first few days one girl has had her eye pierced, another her eye badly scratched... since then 14 accidents have happened in the clock room and corridors through unguarded pins'. Hat pin protectors were made available for sale at 1d each.

1993: a new Polo production line at Rowntree's. We have Nazi Germany to blame for delaying the launch of Polo Mints when they invaded Poland in 1939. The 'mint with a hole' was scheduled for launch in late 1939, but the outbreak of war scuppered the manufacturer's plans. Polo Mints are a breath mint whose defining feature is manufactured in the UK in 1948, invented by employee John Bargewell at the Rowntree Factory in York – a range of flavours (Polo Fruits) followed. The name is a play on 'polar', conjuring up the cool, fresh taste of the mint.

These are the Polo's vital statistics: all Polos are 1.9 centimetres (0.75 in) in diameter and 0.4 centimetres (0.16 in) thick, with a 0.8-centimetre (0.31 in)-wide hole. The word 'POLO' is embossed twice on the upper flat side of the ring, hence the popular slogan 'The Mint with the Hole'. Polos are usually sold in individual packs of twenty-three mints. Its global success is predicated on something that does not exist: that hole in the middle.

Three photographs showing the derelict Rowntree building awaiting redevelopment. Photographs by Exploring The North @exploringthenortheast.

York Carriageworks

Workers at York Carriageworks in the early days. Large premises were built in 1884 around Holgate Road when it was decided to concentrate more carriage building at York: the 1890s and early 1900s saw the Great Carriage Building Programme.

...and in 1988 on the production line. Holgate was an integrated carriage building factory, with separate buildings for each process; by 1910 the works covered forty-five acres. The site comprised two Erecting shops; Patternmakers shop; Paint shop; Cylinder shop; Fitting shop; Machine shop; Cylinder shop; Coppersmiths' shop; Boiler shop; Blacksmiths' shop; Foundry; and Brass finishers. During World War I, one marvelous production was the ambulance train made from existing carriage rolling stock; it comprised sixteen carriages and was known as 'Continental Ambulance Train Number 37'.

Asbestos spraying in 1976. In 1975 an inquest into the death of former railway worker Frank Summers recorded that he had died from an industrial disease; he had previously been employed in asbestos spraying. At the inquest it was claimed that the use of asbestos at the works ended in 1964; initially the dangers of asbestos were not known and employees worked without facemasks or other protection; workers continued to be exposed to asbestos into the 1970s; relatives of workers also developed asbestos related diseases through contact

with dust on workers' clothing. The Holgate Road site was still contaminated with asbestos in the 1990s. By 2012 it was estimated that over 140 workers had died as a result of exposure to asbestos.

Tracks being removed after the closure of York Carriageworks in 2002.

The Royal Mail

18 December 1991 – the travelling Post Office.

Sorting the mail in
Leeman Road.

Marks & Spencer Penny Bazaar, 15-17 Parliament Street.

J.B. Richardson – all leather goods, including portmanteaux, harnesses and whips. The shop was on the corner of Lord Mayor's Walk at Monk Bar; later it was Bulmer's.

The sadly missed Scott's, the famous pork butcher's in Low Petergate in 1992. It closed in 2008, citing gormless council bureaucracy and selfish corporate customers' debts for the decision. Scott's Butchers had been serving York for 130 years.

Some of the staff in 1985.

The human sausage machine at the other go-to pork butchers: Wrights of York, with numerous shops in the city and a factory in Skelton. Famous for their pork pies, sausage rolls, polony and penny ducks. Shops included Bridge Street, Acomb, Bedern, Clifton, Whip-ma-Whop-ma-gate and Blossom Street.

Coney Street in the 1950's. The place to go for your servants.

At any one time there are always people who, for one reason or another, cannot get or hold down work. This image of the Employment Exchange in Parliament Street reminds us of that.

Bookselling in York

Arthur Andersons (Southeran's), Booksellers was in Coney Street in 1837, just one in a long line of York booksellers stretching back to Francis Hildyard's shop established *'at the sign of* The Bible*, Stonegate'* in 1682

In 1763 this became John Todd and Henry Sotheran until 1774 when Sotheran set up on his own next to St Helen's church soon moving across the Square to where the Savings Bank was. Henry Cave's late 18th century Todd's Book and Print Warehouse, as with many booksellers of the time, was something of an apothecary too with a popular line in rat poison, negus and lemonade and similar preparations and confections. Roman busts watched over the 30,000 or so books. William Alexander was another bookseller, in Castlegate; Ann Alexander was the author of a pamphlet campaigning against the exploitation of children and specifically against the employment of climbing boys in 1817. The Book Saloon at 6 Micklegate stocked *'the largest and best selection in the North of England'*, according to *York in 1837*, which goes on to tell us that the bookshop *'meets the demand for healthy literature engendered by the rapid growth of education and educational facilities'*. Thomas Wilson at the Dryden's Head – Bookseller, Stationer, Printer Etc sold fancy goods, local guidebooks and postcards in Coney Street, before that in High Ousegate and Pavement, and Cash Stationery Store in Bridge Street offered *'a wide range of funeral cards'*.

John Glaisby's bookshop and library was in Coney Street, not far from where Waterstones is today.

Thomas Godfrey was a phrenologist who invented his qualifications; he opened his first bookshop at 46½ Stonegate in 1895 selling second hand books *'recently purchased from private libraries'*. The business was called ' Ye Olde Boke Shoppe' but it failed: Godfrey *'became dissatisfied of the apathy of the citizens and disposed of the business'* – sentiments and actions which could be echoed by many an independent bookseller today. An alternative report, though, attributes his failure to the selling of Oscar Wilde's *Portrait of Dorian Gray* after it had been recalled by the publishers thus giving *'offence to some of the good people in York by his handling of a book which was regarded at the time as a most indecent publication'*. Godfrey tried again in 1904 at 37 Goodramgate with the Eclectic Book Company, eventually moving back to 16 Stonegate with a business imaginatively named The Book Company, later Edward S. Pickard. In 1982 the business moved over the road to 32 Stonegate and acquired a second shop on the campus at York University.

John Wolstenholme sold books in Minster Gates, his building graced by his brother's fine statue of Minerva.

Minerva, in Minster gates opposite the top of Stonegate, was the Roman goddess of the arts, culture and learning and symbolizes the literary aura of the area.

The 'Printer's Devil' effigy at 33 Stonegate at the corner of Coffee Yard has been glaring down on us since the 1880s and signifies the importance and prevalence of the printing, bookselling and publishing industries in the area. A printer's devil was a printer's apprentice, a facto-tum. Printing was commonly known as '*the black art*' on account of the inks.

Coffee Yard today

Other evidence for this bookish aspect of York society and commerce are the red Printer's Devil and Coffee Yard off Stonegate. Today, independent bookselling survives with the Little Apple near the Minster.

SCHOOLS &
HOSPITALS

A summer school for contemporary guitar held at the Mount School, August 1979. The story of The Mount School begins with Esther Tuke, second wife of William Tuke, who in 1785 opened the boarding school in Trinity Lane, off Micklegate and known then as the Friends' Girl School. In 1796 purpose-built premises were bought for £450 in Tower Street near to York Castle and the Friends' Meeting House. In 1855 the lease on Castlegate expired, thus triggering the move to the purpose-built buildings at the Mount under the supervision of Rachel Tregelles. Lydia Rous took over as superintendent in 1866 and it was she who ensured that Mount girls entered the new public examinations. The University of London was not interested; to them *girls were poorly educated and therefore incapable of taking a degree course* but Cambridge University, which established Emily Davies' Girton

College for women in 1873, took them on board. Alumni include actors Mary Ure and Dame Judi Dench; the three Drabble sisters: writers A. S. Byatt and Margaret, and art historian Helen Langdon; astronomer Jocelyn Bell Burnell; and TV news correspondent Kathy Killick.

10 November 1989 – Villagers in Copmanthorpe fight to save the breeding ground of the great crested newt in Weavers Close, where new homes were planned.

May 1983: York Minster Song schoolboys were not their usual restrained selves as they shouted encouragement to their friends who were battling it out on the greasy pole at their garden fete. Timothy Munns, left, and Edward Radcliffe are seen here exchanging blows.

Football for the Minster School boys, with a backdrop to die for. Photo courtesy of John Roden originally published in his *The Minster School, York: A Centenary History 1903-2004.*

Non-choristers misbehaving in a singing lesson at the Minster School in 1975.

The Minster School was formerly known as the Minster Song School; Alcuin (c. AD 732-804) was a master here. It specialised in music and singing: of the 180 or so pupils, forty were choristers at York Minster. In addition to singing the early choristers had to read lessons, carry the cross and candles in procession, swing censers, see to the numerous changes of cope for the celebrant during the mass and hold the *Book* for the gospeller. There were three rows of seats, or forms – giving us the derivation of 'forms', as in school desk. In 1903 Dean Purey-Cust made arrangements for a vacant building in Minster Yard to be used as the new song school. Before Deangate was closed to traffic in 1989 pupils were obliged to doff their caps at motorists who allowed them to cross the road en route to the Minster.

Astronomy at Bootham School. Bootham Natural History Society was started in 1834. Its full name was 'The Natural History, Literary and Polytechnic Society' and as such was the umbrella organisation for many other clubs. The Quaker school was evacuated to Roman Catholic Ampleforth during World War II; Donald Gray, the head at the time, is reputed to have addressed the combined school as *'Friends, Romans and Countrymen'*. Bootham was not the only boys' Quaker School in York: in 1827 the Hope Street British School was established and attended by many children of Friends; it was slightly unusual because, in addition to the usual curriculum, it taught the working of the Electric Telegraph with the Electric Telegraph Company supplying the instruments and the school reciprocating by supplying the company with clerks. Image courtesy of Bootham School.

In 1899 almost the entire school was destroyed by fire: a keen pupil was boiling snail shells in the Natural History room when he was summoned by the bell for reading, and the snails were left boiling all night... on being informed by the

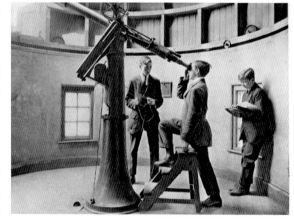

fire brigade that his school was a smouldering shell the headmaster fell on his sword and promptly resigned. The accidental arsonist later became a farmer and blew himself up while uprooting a tree.

Hospitals

York was nothing if not well served by hospitals in the Middle Ages, with at least thirty-one. The most important, and biggest, was St Leonard's. One of the earliest was St Nicholas' leper hospital. St. Giles in Gillygate, was set up before 1274. There was a hospital at Ouse Bridge in the thirteenth century, a Maison Dieu, originally catering for the poor and lepers. St. Mary's Hospital was in Bootham. York had at least four medieval leper hospitals, or lazar-houses; in the 1990s York Archaeological trust rediscovered the site of the 1108 Augustinian leper hospital of St Nicholas in Lawrence Street; excavations uncovered an aisled hall. St. Mary Magdalene was at the end of Bootham just past the Burton Stone; another was near Monkbridge, called St Leonard or St Loy. St Katherine was outside the city beyond Micklegate.

Parked on Deangate, this ambulance is how we used to be taken to the local infirmary. This York motor ambulance, no DN4114, was first registered in April 1921 and sold by Frank Ernest Wasling who ran had three businesses in Blake Street: a cafe, his wife's milliners' shop and the City Garage at 22-23. The garage business began as a cycle shop where he also built bikes. The cars came later; Frank was the Ford dealer in York.

Fulford Open Air School originally opened at 11 Castlegate in 1913 in the same building as the Tuberculosis Dispensary (seen here); it moved in 1914 to a converted army hut in the grounds of Fulford House and became known as Fulford Road School for Delicate and Partially Sighted Children. The open air school movement was set up in 1904 in Berlin to curb the progression of tuberculosis in children and, as such, required the establishment of schools that combined medical care with teaching adapted to pupils with pre-tuberculosis. Fulford closed in 1960 and was demolished in 1964. The Holgate Bridge School for Mentally Defective Boys was opened in 1911 and moved to Fulford House, later known as Fulford Road School for Educationally Sub-Normal Children, in 1923. Photograph: Melvin Browne.

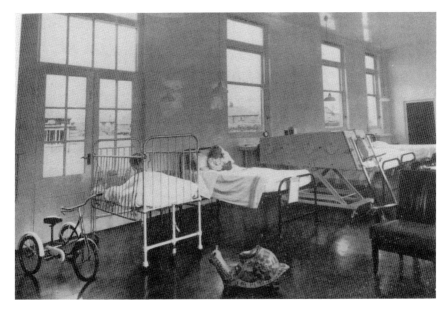

The children's ward at Yearsley Grove Hospital, 1950. The ward is scattered with toys, and contains an 'iron lung' for patients suffering from polio. This was the old 'Fever Hospital' on Huntington Road, near Yearsley Bridge. The earliest hospital buildings date from 1879-81 and came with cast-iron verandas, where patients would sit imbibing the fresh air. In the early years the patients were mainly those suffering from scarlet fever and smallpox. The hospital also looked after patients with typhoid and diphtheria. It was enlarged over time and by the 1930s and 1940s patients with many other infectious diseases were treated here. It became part of the NHS in 1948 and was renamed Yearsley Bridge Hospital. Lisa @YorkStories posted these poignant patient stories:

12 August 2012 from Penny Flack

I spent 6 weeks in the fever hospital in 1961 suffering from scarlet fever and suspected rheumatic fever. I was 11 years old and the only other patient in the huge ward I was in was another girl at the far end. My parents had to walk from Heworth to visit me and could only stay 30 minutes. My two brothers were not allowed in and I lay on the floor and talked to them through the ventilation grills. I seemed to be there a very long time it was so quiet and lonely, no TVs or radios and no staff who had time to chat or play. Near the end of my stay a large group of children patients arrived from a hospital in Hull (I think), moved to York to avoid a polio outbreak. When I got home after 6 long weeks my house seemed very small and cramped.

bagnall1928@yahoo.com 25 August 2012

It was not a pleasant building. My son had this and was taken in, we couldn't go in and see him, just look at him from an outside window. It was a long 3 weeks and made quite a difference when small children could hardly remember their parents when they finally returned home. Scarlet fever was an unpleasant illness for a child and my son was traumatised when he came home and did not know me for some days.

Suzanne 9 March 2013

I was in the fever hospital aged 5 in 1957, I had scarlet fever, and remember going to hospital wrapped in a bright red blanket and being carried into a waiting ambulance. I was the youngest child of 6, and was put on a ward with an open fire with a guard round it, I remember being strapped into bed and having nightmares. I also remember my mum having to wave to me through the window, after she had taken two buses to reach the hospital. I used to enjoy a ride on the rocking horse that we passed on the way back to the ward after being bathed.

An unusual but nevertheless interesting photograph showing the laundry at Clifton Hospital; unusual because a hospital visit rarely, if ever, involves a visit to the laundry. Clifton Hospital opened in April 1847 and closed in July 1994; architect was George Gilbert Scott and others; previous names were North and East Ridings Asylum, and the North Riding of Yorkshire County Mental Hospital from 1920. In 1851 a fire destroyed the original laundry which had to be wholly rebuilt. In 1868 male and female epileptic and suicidal wards were added. York had become one of the centres of excellence in the early development of mental healthcare in England before the Lunacy act of 1895. The city was already home to the York Lunatic Asylum, established in 1777 and the Quaker Retreat, opening in 1796 in reaction to the dubious quality of treatment provided at the earlier authority. The surrounding area also boasted many private madhouses where accommodation was provided for fee-paying lunatics. The 1895 Lunacy act required authorities in the area to provide accommodation for pauper lunatics who had previously been housed in various madhouses and workhouses as well as at York Lunatic Asylum. The district laundry survived the closure of the hospital but closed in the early 2000's and was subsequently demolished with its site used for the new Clifton Park NHS treatment centre.

The magnificent interior of Bootham Park Hospital aka York Lunatic Asylum in 1993 – but you probably wouldn't want to be a patient there. Bootham is designed in the manner of a grand country house, reflecting architect John Carr's experience in designing large Palladian country houses such as Harewood. A major late-C19 refurbishment was undertaken to a notably high level of quality and craftsmanship redolent of a hotel rather than a hospital. Hotel California then? You can check out but...

When Bootham Park opened it was reported in the press as 'an elegant and expensive affair', but William Mason, a Precentor at the Minster, wrote that its extravagant design was a waste of public money and suggested it should instead be advertised as 'a lunatic hotel'. It was later revealed that despite its grandiose exterior some patients were detained in horrific squalor and oppression. Indeed, the conditions at the asylum were the stimulus for the foundation of the The Retreat at York which became world renowned for its pioneering treatment of the mentally ill.

Built to John Carr's design, Bootham Park opened in 1777 with fifteen patients rising to 199 by 1813; its mission was to be caring *'without undue severity'*. Part of the asylum burnt down in 1814 with the tragic loss of four patients, and patient records; somewhat convenient, perhaps, as the fire coincided with a public enquiry and allegations levelled at the management of the asylum, and with the rise of the Retreat, a very different type of psychiatric hospital. All staff were dismissed and replaced. In the same year a visiting magistrate had reported that the *'house is yet in a shocking state... a number of secret cells in a state of filth horrible beyond description'* and the floor covered *'with straw perfectly soaked with urine and excrement'*. In 1904 it was renamed Bootham Park Hospital. In 1777, it was only the fifth purpose-built asylum in the country. One of the founders was Dr Alexander Hunter, the hospital's only physician for many years. His publications include *The Medical History of Worms*.

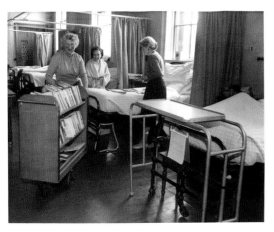

York County Hospital: the photo shows the excellent and invaluable book trolley service in 1962. York County Hospital opened in a rented house in 1740 in Monkgate. Before that, from 1614, the City Surgeon was responsible for medical care. In 1745 a purpose-built hospital opened on the same site with fifty beds: by 1750 2,417 patients had been treated. One of the stipulations of the hospital was that prospective patients must pay a deposit on admission to cover burial fees – refundable only if you walked out alive. As a charitable hospital (where the financiers could choose who received treatment there) the County Hospital was not responsible for the city's sick poor; this led to the establishment of the Dispensary. The 1745 hospital building was demolished in 1851 and replaced with a new 100 bed hospital costing £11,000. In 1887 it merged with the York Eye Institution, opened in 1875. The present York District Hospital opened in 1976 replacing the County Hospital, Fulford Hospital, Deighton Grove Hospital, Yearsley Bridge Hospital, Acomb Hospital, the Military Hospital and City Hospital. The 18th century also saw the founding of York Lunatic Asylum (Bootham Park) and the revolutionary, enlightened Retreat for the humane care of the mentally ill.

The new ante-natal clinic at York County Hospital in 1963.

A garden party at York Maternity Hospital (later Acomb Hospital) in what used to be Acomb Hall in September 1944. Acomb Hospital was housed in a former private house called Acomb Hall, which was acquired by York Corporation and officially opened as a maternity hospital on 19 December 1922, replacing the first York Maternity Hospital 1908-1922 run by York Dispensary at 15 Ogleforth. The hospital continued the work of its predecessor in training pupil midwives. About a dozen midwives were trained each year in the 1920s, rising to about 20 each year in the 1930s and around 30 each year in the 1940s and early 1950s. In the late 1940s and early 1950s about 60% of births in York were institutional (private nursing homes between them providing a further 30 or so maternity beds) and around 40% were domiciliary. The hospital closed on 25 October 1954 when services were transferred to the much larger Fulford Maternity Hospital. However, the building, renamed Acomb Hospital, reopened as a geriatric hospital on 25 November 1954.

The York Union Workhouse in the 1900s. Built by the Atkinsons and completed probably in 1849, this was eventually taken over by York Corporation in 1930 and became the York City Hospital. In 1551, part of St Anthony's Hall, one of York's Houses of Correction at the time, was used as a poorhouse. In 1567 and

1569, two weaving establishments were established for the unemployed in St Anthony's Hall and St George's House, but the goods they produced were useless. After many unsuccessful attempts a number of the city's parishes set up a joint workhouse in 1768 to accommodate ninety paupers in a former cotton factory at 26 Marygate, again, working with textiles. York Poor Law Union was established in 1837 and took over Marygate: hygiene left much to be desired, according to this 1839 inspection, after an outbreak of food poisoning from a vat of soup:

> 'In a room, however, in my opinion as a Chemist, ill adapted for the purpose of preserving meat, we found a Beast's Head at that time offensive to the smell... This room adjoins and opens into a short and very narrow yard considerably tainted with all the effluvia rising from some privies at one end... The head not having been previously cleaned, a quantity of unwholesome mucus was attached to it.'

The Guardians nevertheless concluded that the soup had made inmates ill because 'the usual quantity of Potatos [sic] had been omitted making the soup too strong and rich'. The Poor Law Commissioners recommended a replacement for the Marygate workhouse reporting 'a permanent reservoir of foul air'; and the privies were 'without exception in an offensive state'. Most of the inmates were 'children, the aged and infirm and persons of weak mind'; many, if not all, were diseased and children mixed 'in the infectious wards with adults labouring under syphilis and gonorrhea'. The paupers mocked the idiots 'as a pastime'. In August 1845, the Leeds Mercury reported on the women's ward in an official inspection: 'this place is used by aged idiots, women and children, and besides being of limited extent, it has only one privy, with an open cesspool. In 1849 a new union workhouse was built on Huntington Road housing 300 inmates. Different inmates were separated by a network of walls, including one specifically for unmarried women and one for 'female idiots'. There was also a washhouse, laundry, and the mortuary. On the men's side were an oakum-picking shop, carpenter's shop, stone yard, and a coach-house. In 1930, the workhouse became a Public Assistance Institution, while part of the building became York City Hospital. In 1946, it was renamed the Grange, and in 1955 became St Mary's Hospital. This closed in the late 1970s and the buildings were converted to student accommodation.

Fairfield Sanatorium was the first tuberculosis (TB) sanatorium to be opened by York Corporation. York had considered acquiring a small estate to be operated as a TB farm colony, which would also take advanced cases and accommodate open air workshops. This would also relieve the growing pressure on existing TB beds at Yearsley Bridge Fever Hospital. In 1918 the Corporation purchased a large Georgian house and a site of 100 acres about two miles north of the city; in the 1800's it was an estate for trading and breeding horses. The house was converted to TB accommodation by the Corporation, and was named Fairfield Sanatorium. Local Government Board approval was conditional on the sanatorium being available on a priority basis to discharged military personnel.

In 1961 the name was changed to 'Fairfield Hospital' to reflect the fact that it would now serve a variety of functions: child psychiatric, and general chest cases as well as TB. The hospital closed in 1976 and subsequently became the hotel we see in the photograph.

Field Gun training at the Ordnance Depot in Hospital Fields, with the Military Hospital behind the fence. Probably during World War I. Image from the Geoff Shearsmith Collection, courtesy of FFH.

In 1918 the *Yorkshire Herald* reported:

On Friday September 6th, 1918, a convoy of 160 wounded soldiers arrived by train into York City Station at 3.30am. They were met by members of the

newly formed Women's Department of Stretcher Bearers, who, under the supervision of Colonel F.W. Lamballe, assisted in the transport of 30 men to York County Hospital. A further 50 men were sent to the Central Military Hospital on Fulford Road, which extended its buildings to meet this additional demand. The largest group of 80 soldiers were transferred to the Haxby Road Military Hospital.

Haxby Road Military Hospital was set up in the dining block of the Rowntree's chocolate factory. It had 200 beds, along with emergency care for soldiers and citizens injured in France and Belgium. The Friends Ambulance Unit ran the hospital, a Quaker voluntary service founded to provide non combatant service opportunities for pacifist conscientious objectors. The photo shows patients recovering at the hospital.

V.A.D. (Voluntary Aid Detachment) hospitals

VADs and staff at Nunthorpe Hall 1918. Nunthorpe V.A.D. hospital was in the area now known as Coggan Close, between Albemarle Road and Philadelphia Terrace; it opened on the 1st October 1915 with 50 beds taken by a convoy of men direct from the battle of Loos. The eccentric but philanthropic Sir Edward Green gave over his house to the V.A.D., to be run by his daughter in law, Lycett Green; between them they bore all expenses not covered by the government grant. Nursing staff included one matron and three sisters, one sister was qualified to apply therapeutic massage. Matron and two sisters lived in. There were 24 VADs, two cooks and two charwomen. The hall was bombed by Zeppelin in 1916 with two bombs setting fire to the house and four falling in the garden. There was considerable damage and the hospital had to be evacuated. It closed in 1919 after treating 914 patients and was demolished in 1977. Photo of Nunthorpe Hall from *West Riding St. John Ambulance War Service* by CME Duncombe, no date.

Clifford Street V.A.D hospital was in the Friends meeting house opened 1915, with a convoy of soldiers direct from the Front. It started with 40 beds which were later increased to 56. It closed January 1919. The number of patients treated was 819.

YORK CULTURE & ENTERTAINMENT

Paul McCartney signs autographs outside The Rialto. The Beatles played in York four times: February 27 1963, March 13 1963, May 29 1963, and finally November 27 1963 – all at the Rialto in Fishergate.

They came in through the bathroom window. The Beatles at the Rialto, 1963.

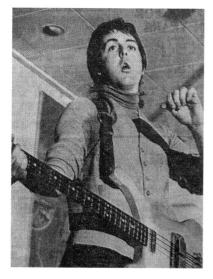

Nine years later Paul McCartney was back for an impromptu performance at Goodricke College dining room, University of York on Thursday, 10 February 1972. Photo credit: https://www.the-paulmccartney-project.com/concert/1972-02-10/

The March 1963 concert poster.

At York's Rialto in February 1963, Paul McCartney and Ringo Starr are seen with co-manager of the Rialto John Hattersley-Colson, and Brian Epstein. On at least one occasion the Beatles stayed at the Edinburgh Arms.

York Repertory Company in 1955 in a production of *When We Are Married*. The *York Evening Press* photographer is behind the drunk photographer acting in the play (J. Barrie).

Again in 1959 with John Tinn as the Japanese soldier, James Beck on the right and Trevor Bannister in *The Long and the Short and the Tall*.

152

A 1969 Theatre Royal production of *A Christmas Carol.*

The first York theatre was built on tennis courts in Minster Yard in 1734 by Thomas Keregan. In 1744 his widow built The New Theatre here on what was the city's Mint, itself built on the site of St. Leonard's Hospital. In 1765 it was rebuilt by Joseph Baker and enlarged to seat 550, *'by far the most spacious in Great Britain, Drury Lane and Covent Garden excepted',* according to the *York Courant.* Access to the site of the Mint can still be gained from the back of the main stage. During the 1760's a small theatre also existed: the Little Theatre, in Jubbergate, where the Leeds Company of Comedians were performing *The Beaux' Stratagem* and other plays in 1767. At this time York's main theatre was illegal and it was not until a Royal Patent was granted in 1769 and the theatre was renamed the Theatre Royal that this status changed. Gas lighting came in 1824 and in 1835 a new frontage was built facing onto the newly created St. Leonard's Place. This was removed to Fulford Road in 1880 and replaced with a new facade. The 'encore!' had its premiere in York, at the Theatre Royal in 1791 after a performance of the *Conjuror's Song* in which a leg of lamb, a cake and a lawyer in a sack were conjured up. The audience enjoyed this so much that they demanded to see it again – a somewhat difficult request. Performers and orchestra left the stage amid a salvo of candles and candlesticks: the audience was only placated when the orchestra returned to play the song again. York Theatre Royal was the venue in 1853 for a concert by Miss Greenfield, a black, former slave girl; reviews in the *Yorkshire Gazette* were very favourable. There is a Roman well under the stage.

1979's controversial production of *Oh What a Lovely War* by Joan Littlewood.

"A touch of Paris in the centre of York," reads the *Press's* original caption, after magistrates allowed a three-week trial of an outdoor cafe in the Theatre Royal forecourt.

Kit Surrey working on the backcloths for the Theatre Royal production of *Lord Byron Lives*, January 1971.

Shed Seven frontman Rick Witter (left) encourages a little intimate crowd participation in the first of the three consecutive nights at Fibbers in York. Previous names of Fibbers include Ellingtons and Fazers Fun pub.

1985 – The Clash strut down Petergate on May 9, 1985 after an impromptu performance outside the Minster – and then on to King's Square for another quick busk:

The Clash busking.

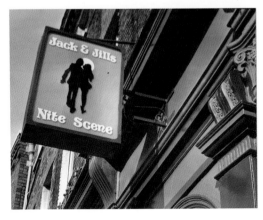

1972 – Jack & Jills in Bootham.

Some well known faces at the York Waxwork Museum in Friargate. Janet Bowen offers tea to, from left, the Queen, Princess Anne and Princess Diana in the 1980s. Princess Anne looks none too pleased.

April 1988 saw a dalek causing traffic mayhem in Tower Street – an escapee from the Museum of Automaton.

'The Ardath' (floating) club alongside Terry Avenue in 1972.

'The Ardath' (sinking). You wouldn't know it now if you walked along Terry Avenue, just downstream from Skeldergate Bridge – but this was once a vibrant venue in York's music and drinking scenes. When planning permission was renewed in 1972, councillors praised its interior and said it was a good tourist attraction for York.

Veteran York pantomimer, Berwick Kaler, had announced that the 2020 pantomime *Dick Turpin Rides Again* will now be moved to Christmas 2021 at the Grand Opera House. The buildings that today house the Grand Opera House were never intended to be a theatre. The tall section was built as York's Corn Exchange in 1868 with plans to use it occasionally as a concert hall. The auditorium was originally a warehouse opening onto Kings Street. In 1902 when the Corn Exchange failed, the buildings were converted by William Peacock. The theatre opened on January 20th, 1902 with *Little Red Riding Hood* starring Florrie Ford. In 1903 the name was changed to The Grand Opera House and Empire because new regulations banned smoking in theatres but permitted it in music halls. It stayed with William Peacock's family until 1945; performers included Charlie and Sydney Chaplin, Gracie Fields, Lillie Langtry, George Robey, Cecily Courtneidge and Jimmy Jewel. From 1945 – 1956 F.J. Butterworth owned the theatre and stars such as Vera Lynn, Laurel and Hardy and Morecome and Wise appeared. In 1958 Shepherd of the Shambles bought it, and it became the SS Empire. The stage, lower boxes and raked stall floor were removed and replaced by a large flat floor suitable for roller-skating, dancing, bingo and wrestling. In 1987 new owners the India Pru Co. Ltd spent £4,000,000 restoring it to its former glory.

Snow White and the Seven Dwarfs at the Grand Opera House 2019-2020. This is Three Bears Productions' fourth Grand Opera House pantomime, written, directed and co-produced by Chris Moreno.

Another club floating on the Ouse – this is the 'Flying Dutchman' in 1984.

YORK AT WAR

First World War nurse Ursula Lascelles was nominated in a 2020 *York Press* search for 'Great North Yorkshire sons and daughters'. Voluntary Aid Detachment (VAD) nurse Ursula Lascelles travelled from Slingsby to the battlefields of France. She was born in Sheriff Hutton in July 1890, and died in 1992, aged 102. Ursula was the daughter of the vicar of Sheriff Hutton and was educated at the girls' grammar school in York. At the outbreak of World War One, Ursula, then 24, and her mother, Elizabeth, volunteered as VAD nurses. Ursula began volunteering at the British Red Cross Hospital in Swinton Grange, near Malton. She volunteered to nurse on the frontline in France and in 1917 she was posted to the No.6 General Hospital in Rouen, France, where she worked as a VAD nurse until 1919. After the war, and throughout her life, Ursula continued to fundraise for the British Red Cross. Her influence on the patients she treated is evident in the records held at the County Record Office. The Lascelles family collection includes hundreds of letters from soldiers she looked after thanking Ursula for her care. Ursula kept in contact with many soldiers after the war. Although Ursula came from a privileged background, she dedicated her life to supporting those in need and less fortunate than herself.

On February 1st, 1945, J.E. Mcdonald was the first of 600 airmen to scratch their names on the mirror downstairs at Bettys during World War II. Also known as Bettys Bar or the Dive it was a regular haunt of the hundreds of airmen

stationed in and around York; these included many Canadians from Number 6 Bomber Group. One signatory, Jim Rogers, borrowed a waitress' diamond ring to scratch his name on the mirror.

York Home Guard reviving the historical purpose of the city walls by using them as a last line of defence of the city. Photo from *The York Blitz 1942* by Eric Taylor and Leo Kessler (York 1986).

The Home Guard securing Lendal Bridge. Photo from *The York Blitz 1942.*

York civil defence volunteers in World War II. York was hit by 11 raids between 17 August 1940 and 17 December 1942. 295 people were injured in the raids and 99 people died during the raids. 2,828 people were made homeless thanks to the 235 bombs dropped on York damaging or destroying 9,500 houses. According to research by 'Raids over York'

In total, 2,554 ordinary people risked their lives as Air Raid Wardens, medical orderlies, and firewatchers in York as part of the civil defence of their city; finishing their daytime jobs and duties, then donning their Civil Defence service helmets or grabbing their medical kits and heading out on Civil Defence duty, often until the early hours and regardless of how bad the weather was.

The following details are extracted from 'Raids over York', https://raidsovery-ork.co.uk/raid2-28-oct-1940/

Raid #1 (11 Aug. 1940)

According to Air Raid Precaution [A.R.P] Warden's report, the first bomb to fall in York as one of the 10 targeted raids (a chance bomb fell a week or so earlier), did so at 10.12pm. It is thought that the unidentified Luftwaffe bomber that dropped the bombs was intended for a raid on Sheffield. Rather ironically the first bomb exploded close to the WW1 'Cross of Sacrifice' in York Cemetery. "A further bomb fell in the Kensall Rise area… [damaging] the water service… and a crater was located by the Police and several bomb fragments recovered. Superficial damage was again caused to house property. Two slight casualties were reported from this incident, who were injured by flying glass. The bomb is estimated at approximately 112 lbs [50Kgs]". 80 properties in nearby Cemetery Road also had their windows blown out, rooftiles dislodged, and chimneys toppled, with some receiving "quite extensive damage to roofs, window frames, doors, ceilings and walls". Further bombs during that raid fell nearby in Edgware Road, Heslington Road, and an unexploded bomb in the River Foss near the Castle Museum, which the Royal Engineers later "estimated to be sunk about 30 feet in the river bed and… not a danger". [Is it still there?!] There were two minor casualties who were treated as 'out patients' and one serious casualty requiring hospital treatment.

Raid #2 (28 Oct. 1940)

Part of a sustained raid over the North-East of England. Four high-explosive bombs were dropped near Haxby Moor with the Co-op in the village rumoured to have been machine-gunned by a low flying enemy aircraft. At 22:27, a "stick" of four, high-explosive bombs were dropped in the Malton Road area. The first bomb fell in the farmyard of "Thorn Nook" – now demolished and incorporated by modern housing – but then just off Elmfield Avenue. The third bomb fell in the front garden of 11 Sefton Avenue, creating a ten-foot-wide crater and doing 'superficial damage to house property' for the length of 100 yards on either side of the street and affecting 30 "semis" (later considered 'extensive damage' in the Police report). 'Not a single pane of glass was left intact, and in many instances the window frames also were smashed', according to *The Yorkshire Post*. Tragically two men were killed here: John Thomas March and Henry Coles. John was 34 years old, lived at No.9 Sefton Avenue, and was on duty then as a part-time Air-Raid Warden. He was killed instantly, taking the full force of the explosion. Henry, who lived at No.22 Sefton Avenue, and was 59 years old, received a fatal wound to the upper chest area and was also killed instantly.

18 January 1939 – The Princess Royal pouring out tea for soldiers at York Station Canteen. The Princess Royal was Mary, Princess Royal and Countess of Harewood (1897 – 1965). During World War II she was Controller Commandant of the Auxiliary Territorial Service.

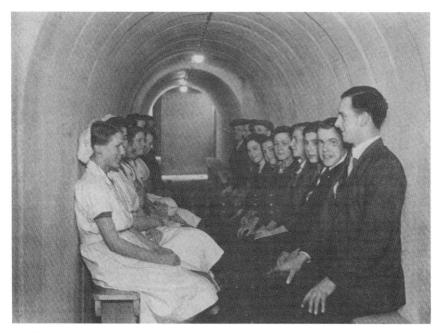

Workers inside one of Rowntree's air-raid shelters during a practice drill. *Cocoa Works Magazine* Easter 1939.

The Baedeker Raid, April 28th, 1942

The raids on York, Norwich, Bath, Canterbury and Exeter became known as Baedeker Raids because Hermann Göring's staff allegedly used the famous travel guide to select their *Vergeltungsangriffe* (retaliatory) targets – namely 3 star rated English cities – in retaliation for the RAF's destruction of the Hanseatic league towns of Lübeck and Rostock. The attack of 28 March 1942 on Lübeck created a firestorm that caused severe damage to the historic centre. The German police reported 301 people dead, three people missing, and 783 injured. More than 15,000 people lost their homes.

The bombed cathedral at Lübeck. German Federal Archives.

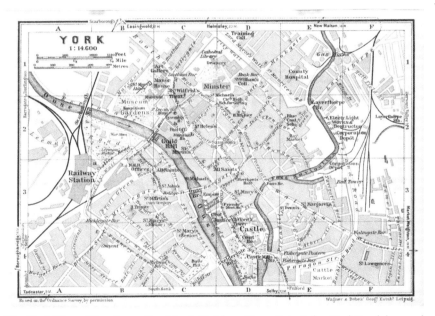

The York Town Plan from *Baedeker's Guide to Great Britain* by Karl Baedeker and published by Wagner & Debes Geographical Establishment, Leipzig 1937. This innocuous map would have formed the basis for Luftwaffe intelligence relating to ground liaison for the raid.

One bomb load of high explosives and incendiaries fell in a line from New Street, through the Leopard Arcade in Coney Street, St Martin's and the dairy next door, terminating at the medieval Guildhall. Seventy German bombers, largely unopposed, bombed York for two hours: eighty-six York people died including fourteen children, and ninety-eight were seriously injured (not including undisclosed army and RAF fatalities). Six German aircrew perished. It seems that an incendiary bomb smashed through the 19th century east window of the church and lodged in the organ in the north aisle. Normally it might have burnt out, but the organ went up in flames and the fire crews were considerably overstretched. The eight bells of 1719 crashed down. After protracted argument the church was finally restored but not before the damaged bells were stolen around 1960. The new organ was paid for by the German federal government, and the Civic Trust assisted with other work. The surviving south aisle and tower were rebuilt and the church was re-hallowed in April 1968 – with its dedication to peace and reconciliation.

Overall, the church has been described as the best post-war church restoration in the country. The website says it best: *what is there was intended to remind future generations of the loss and wastage of war. We must never forget, and can never forget at St Martin's, the rededication to peace and reconciliation.*

(29th April 1942 Baedeker Raid)

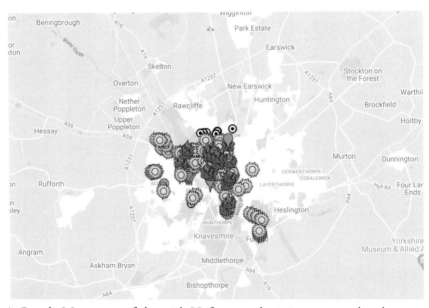

A Google Maps map of the raid. Unfortunately, it is not very clear because the incendiary bomb and high explosive bomb sites literally obliterate all the detail. Nevertheless, it does serve to show the focus of the bombing and its sheer intensity.

9,500 houses (30% of the city's stock) were damaged or destroyed leaving 2,000 people homeless. Five nuns were tragically killed during the 1942 Baedeker Raid. The Bar Convent School was hit by a delayed action bomb. Six of the nuns in residence were firewatchers and stayed above ground when the raid started (the other nuns and pupils having gone down to the shelters). However, when the dust settled Mother Mary Agnes was found to be missing. Some of the nuns went to search for her when she was heard in the rubble below close to the bomb. Unfortunately, as they went for a ladder to rescue her, the bomb exploded and Mother Agnes and all but one of the rescue party were killed. The casualties were Madeline Clayton aged 51 – Sister Mary Agnes (House Prefect); Eva Jordon aged 53 – Sister Mary Vincent (Headmistress, English Martyrs School); Jane McClorry aged 65 – Sister Mary Gerard (Infirmarian); Margaret Murphy aged 50 – Sister Mary Brendan (recently joined from Ascot); Mary Ann O'Connor – aged 39 – Sister Mary Patricia (Teacher in the Junior School). It was not until Sunday 3rd May that all five bodies were recovered.

The full details of that terrible night at the convent can be found at http://bomberhistory.co.uk/assets/pdf/bar_convent_story.pdf

The wrecked Bar Convent.

The day after the raid the *Daily Mail* patriotically reported: '*The gates of York still stand high, like the spirit of its people who, after nearly two hours of intense bombing and machine-gunning, were clearing up today*'. There is a plaque on York Railway Station in honour of Station Foreman William Milner who died in the raid while entering a burning building to get medical supplies. His body was found still holding the box; he was posthumously awarded the King's Commendation for Gallantry. The following 19 images show the destruction that awaited York on that fateful night.

Three residents of 57 Chatsworth Terrace owe their lives to the Morrison Shelter's robust construction

Dousing the flames at the Leopard Arcade in Coney Street opposite St Martin le Grand.

Platform 3 of York Railway Station back in service minus the canopy just three days after the raid. Amazingly, the platform actually re-opened the morning after the raid. LNER official photo passed for publication in 1942.

The Carriageworks roundhouse took a direct hit and all of the twenty engines in there at the time suffered damage. *The Sir Ralph Wedgwood* A4 Pacific (named after the former NER Chief General Manager) was totally destroyed when a bomb blew up in Clifton engine shed. The Leeman Road stables were also struck, necessitating the evacuation of nineteen panicking, and very dangerous, dray horses from the site. The Royal Engineers were called in to help repair the damage to the lines and the station. Photo from *The York Blitz 1942*.

The Guildhall on fire. The hall was built in 1445 on the site of the earlier 'Common Hall' dating from at least 1256. It was originally for the Guild of St Christopher and St George and the Corporation who took over completely in 1549. Council meetings are still held there in the Victorian Council Chamber of 1891. It was used as a theatre – Richard III watched *Credo* here in 1483 – and as a Court of Justice, and was where Margaret Clitherow was tried in 1586. In 1647 during the Civil War, Cromwell agreed to pay a ransom of £200,000 to the Scots in exchange for Charles I; the money was counted here. It contains a bell captured at the Siege of Rangoon in 1851. The Guildhall was badly damaged in the Baedeker Raid of 1942 – at the time it was the oldest Guildhall in England but was fully restored in 1960. The subterranean Common Hall Lane passes under the Guildhall – then called Common Hall, to a jetty on the river, originally a continuation of Stonegate.

Loose change fused together by the heat of the conflagration.

The shell of St Martin-le-Grand in Coney Street.

Day off tomorrow at Poppleton Road Primary School. The Manor Higher Grade, Shipton Street, St Barnabas, Queen Anne Secondary and Nunthorpe Secondary schools and the School of Art were all damaged to some extent.

The Halifax bomber that crashed into York's 'unluckiest street' – Nunthorpe

Grove in South Bank. Picture: Hugh Murray estate. From *Shadows in the Bricks*. In 1942 bombs destroyed four houses and the plane crash in 1945 pictured here resulted in 13 deaths and numerous injuries. Four houses were also set on fire. Workmen repairing roof tiles and ground work to one of the damaged properties in Sefton Avenue after the 28 October raid in 1940. All windows have been 'put in' by the blast, and impact of debris can be seen on the near corner of the property.

German prisoners of war arriving at York station late in the war. They would have been sent to one of the many POW camps in and around York, including Knavesmire (the largest) and what is now Eden Camp. Photo: *The York Blitz 1942*.

AND FINALLY...

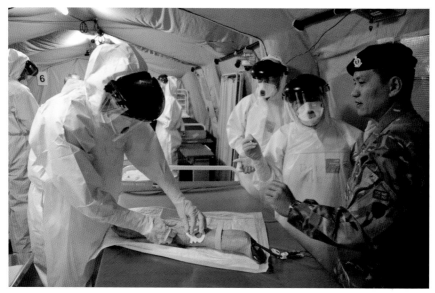

Medical Regiment 250 Sqn RAMC (Detachment) training in blood – taking during the Ebola pandemic. Strensall Queen Elizabeth barracks.

COVID 19 vaccination site

How the people of York have been showing their support for the Ukraine appeal.

BY THE SAME AUTHOR

A History of Britain in 100 Objects

The Rowntrees: The Early History

Old York

A History of Sweets

The History of the World in 100 Pandemics, Plagues and Epidemics

Pubs in and Around York

A Historical Guide to Roman York

The Making of Roman York

Life in York 100 Years Ago

Factory Girls: The Working Lives of Women & Children

Inside the craftsmen shop in Goodramgate looking in in 1966.

ALSO BY THE AUTHOR

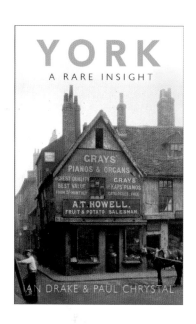

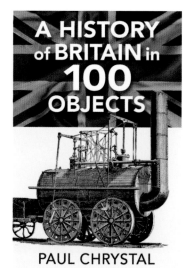